Desert Storm:
and The War Inside Myself

By D. W. (Bill) Moore

D. W. (Bill) Moore, RE
SoulDance LLC
www.OutlawDrummers.com
Olympia, Washington U.S.A.

Copyright © by D.W. Moore

All right reserved. No part of this book may be reproduced in any form, except for brief reviews, without the permission of the Author.

Olympia, WA 98506 USA

Cover Art: © 2014 Bill Moore

SBN-13: 978-1508723691
ISBN-10: 1508723699

First Print, 2015

Also by this author:

RHYTHM HEALING
PTSD Trauma and Beyond
D.W.(BILL) MOORE

Available at Amazon & Kindle

For more information:
www.OutlawDrummers.com
Bill@OutlawDrummers.com

Desert Storm

Me on my Bradley

Just another GI's story

I have been encouraged many times now to write down my story of Desert Shield/ Desert Storm. My reply has always been that I am no hero, just an average Joe, and that no one would want to hear my story. My friends seem to think different and say it would help people get a clearer picture of what it was like from a ground soldier's point of view, the mental damages that can occur under combat stress, living with mental damage after the war and coming out the other side. So, here goes.

Desert Storm

I have heard several people say; you signed up and got what you signed up for, so quit bitching. We humans think of ourselves as smart and think we can see consequences to our actions beforehand. The reality I found is that we don't always take the consequences seriously. Hindsight is 20/20. Yes, I did sign my name, but I don't think there were any of us that went that really thought we would end up in a war and have people trying to kill us. I don't believe it was short sighted thinking, just passive denial. It could happen, it just hasn't happened lately. It happens to other people, just not to me.

Living in a unique country that has not had warfare on its own ground in several life times, causes us to view the world as being a safe, secure place. It is not and never has been. Whether we want to believe it or not, our governing bodies, from the beginning of recorded history, think of war as a game to advance their own agendas. The government's greed for more pushes us into conflict and the average people end up giving their lives for it. That is the world we live in.

It seems natural for most little boys to play war. I know I dreamed of honor, glory, and proving myself as a man in battle;

Desert Storm

protecting my family and friends from the aggressors. Television fed into that image I had in my mind. Living through a war and the aftermath it had on my life was nothing like it was made out to be; it just left me angry and hurting inside.

I grew up in a small town in the mountains of North Idaho. Hunting fed my family every winter. So weapons and killing animals were not new to me. When the war started, I was in my second enlistment of active duty in the military. The first was four years in the Navy straight out of high school. I spent most of the time then on an air base just outside Pensacola, Florida, working on 50's vintage aircraft and soaking up the sun on the beaches. Then, I spent four more years working as a civilian. Those are other stories. I had gone back into the military in 1987 because I was trying to take control of my life. Retiring from the military looked like a good choice at the moment. Four years in the infantry and then I could choose whatever job I wanted. It sounded so easy.

I will start this story from the point of getting to my Army unit which I did combat with. My journey with the 3rd of the 15th

started a year before the war and has relevance to the story. It was a busy year.

The names of most of the participants will be changed to protect the innocent, and some of the events will be toned down for my own comfort. Even though I have worked through a lot of my issues, there still are some tender points that will not be gone into in depth. As the saying goes, "war is hell." I have lived through it and it has changed me forever.

Desert Storm

Hurricane Hugo 1989

My assignment was the 24th Army Infantry Division in Savannah, Georgia; 3rd Battalion, 15th Infantry. I was 29 years old by then. I had just spent two years in Aschaffenburg, Germany with the 2nd Battalion, 7th Infantry. They gave me my Buck Sergeant's stripes, just weeks before I left Germany. Two years from private to sergeant. Not bad for a second enlistment.

Before I could get settled in good at the new base, Hurricane Hugo decided to grace us with its presence. Savannah just caught the edge of it, but Charleston got hit hard. This was my second hurricane in my life. The first had been Hurricane Fredric while I was in the Navy. Our Battalion was picked to help with the relief efforts in Charleston. We followed a construction battalion as they cleared the roads all the way into down town. As a sergeant, I was assigned as a TC (Truck Commander) on a 5 Ton truck for the convoy. Being a TC is like being the responsible adult on board; you're just along for the ride. My driver was a kid from Oregon named Sean. I later found that they put me with him because he was a bit of a problem child and I was the new

Desert Storm

guy. I think that it is an unwritten law, to always dump the problems on the new guy. Sean and I have been friends ever since. The back was loaded with soldiers and equipment. As we got closer to Charleston, we noticed that the trees had been sheared off at the top. And by the time we were down town, the trees and everything else were sheared off at about two story building height. Debris was everywhere. Mother Nature is powerful; the sight of the devastation took my breath away. In Charleston, we were put up in a school gym with no electricity, no cots and cold running water for a month. We all talked shit about how hard we had it down there in the South Carolina late summer weather, but looking back after the war, we had it made and worst of all, I believe we knew it. It was a lot better duty than playing for weeks in the mud of South Georgia for field duty, which was where we would have been.

    I got to know the rest of my new company while unloading trucks, sorting, and sending out supplies for the Red Cross. We worked 12 hours on duty and 12 hours off duty 7 days a week for that month. We had people for weeks coming to us for help; most everyone coming on foot. Some had hiked for days to get there.

Desert Storm

Most people left right away with extra supplies to get them back to people who couldn't walk out. Trucks came to the warehouse we were working out of with food, clothes, and supplies from all over the country. The Red Cross took good care of us and it turned into a great experience of learning and helping others. The kindness and generosity of everyone through the whole ordeal touched my heart. It was one of those rare moments in my life and my military service to my country, that when I was done, I knew I had made a difference in other people's lives for the good. It saddens me to say that that is not a statement that I can make looking back at Desert Storm.

On return from Hugo relief, we got a few days off. I am not sure of exactly why now, maybe because he was the first person I had met in six years of active duty that was from the North West or I just felt sorry for the kid, but I took Sean with me down to Daytona Beach for a couple of days of sun, sand, and frolic. I was not supposed to fraternize with the under ranks and especially not in my platoon, but he was a nice kid and seemed like he just needed some direction. We were told to be mentors for our younger troops. As it turned out, Sean has become one of my

Desert Storm

portals with sanity for the rest of my life. It can be funny how life works sometimes. We find that everyone around us can become our student and our teachers.

All through the fall, I got settled into my job as the Company Armorer. My job involved maintenance and security of all the companies' weapons and ammunition. The Company's CO (Commanding Officer) and Top (Company 1st sergeant) wanted me in an infantry platoon because I was an 11M (Armored Infantry, Bradley) and so far had done mostly Armorer work, and also they didn't seem to like me and wanted more control over me. The Battalion Commander intervened and posted me as the company's Armorer because I already had my Secret Security clearance and I had received an Army Achievement Medal and an Army Commendation medal for running the weapons room in Germany for my last company. As the Armorer, I was part of the Company, but I was directly under the Battalion Commander. In matters of security and maintenance for the weapons, I was over the CO and Top. Needless to say, that did not go over well. I am not going to go into character flaws of either of them, I just want to state that I have had some good people to work for and bad people to work for, and these two were at the top of the worst pile. Even though they tried to play me, I knew what orders they could give me and I also knew that there were some orders I could give to them. It can be fun and problematic playing the edge of "within my duty" and outright belligerence. I don't have much respect for stupid people who use their position to advance their own agenda. I have been told many times that I have problems with authority, if I don't respect the person. Sean said I had it down to an art. Piss them off without them being able to do anything about it. The one thing they couldn't deny was that I did my job to the best of my ability. My first inspection, I got the highest score the battalion had ever gotten. That pretty much locked me into the position of Battalion Arms Room expert. Every other Arms Room had Staff sergeants in charge and did not like having a Buck Sergeant telling them how to do their jobs. That did score some points with Top and the CO, because it made them and the company look good.

Although, any credit I did build up, I used it up getting Sean out of one pissing match after the other with Top. I believed that as Assistant Platoon Sergeant in headquarters platoon, it was

Desert Storm

my job to stand between my troops and Top when they got into trouble, then I would deal with my troops later. That gained me a lot of respect from my soldiers when they knew they could screw up and Sgt. Moore would take the heat for them. I tried to make my punishment for them fit the crime. They would take things from me that they wouldn't take from Top.

In late fall or early winter, we did a two week maneuver through the live firing range in the (BIFV) Bradley Infantry fighting vehicles. For the live fire, each company was taking turns shooting live rounds for the range exercises. Each company only gets to do a live fire twice a year.

The Bradley, for short, resembles a tank, with three crew members. One driver and has a turret which takes two people to handle, the gunner and the BC (Bradley Commander). The gunner runs various weapons such as a 25mm cannon (the big gun on the turret), 3.65mm machine gun and a pair of wire guided tank buster rockets. The 25mm cannon could almost fire as fast as the machine gun. There were four Bradley's in each platoon with three platoons and the CO's, Bradley.

Desert Storm

The BC was usually a Staff Sergeant or higher. It was the officer's position in the command vehicles. The BC runs communications, monitors the driver and is the second pair of eyes for the gunner and the driver. He also sets the course for the vehicle, monitors the gunner's blind spots (which are many), can over-ride the turret controls in case the gunner doesn't see a life threatening target, but he cannot fire a shot. Pulling the trigger is the gunner's job. The BC is a busy person.

The drive sits forward and left on the Bradley. The big difference between a Bradley and a tank is that it is much lighter armored and carries up to six soldiers inside in the rear. The soldiers could be dropped at a moment's notice out a big door in the rear of the Bradley. There were 13 Bradley's in a Company, 12 filled with soldiers, and one command vehicle for the CO which only carried the driver, gunner, and the CO.

Desert Storm

This is a Bradley Infantry Fighting Vehicle. M-2 BIFV

I got put as a TC in a 5 Ton truck with Sean as my driver again. I had two big boxes of repair parts and tools for all the weapons, some extra rifles, and my own gear. Security and maintenance on all the companies' weapons was my first and foremost job. Our second job was to run errands for everybody who was too lazy to do it themselves. I didn't do any actual training. That wasn't too bad, it was kind of cold and the trucks had heaters and we stayed away from Top as much as possible. Nothing really exciting happened for those two weeks of training.

Desert Storm

I did learn that I have never met anyone as directionally challenged as Sean. I used to tease him about getting lost in his own back yard. GPS has become his best friend over the years.

I wrecked my car that winter. I got hit in the driver's side door by a couple of teenage girls who weren't paying attention. My head broke the driver's window and I woke up with the paramedics asking me how many fingers he was holding up. I was wondering where I was and how a paramedic got into my dream. My platoon sergeant came and picked me up from Savannah. I don't remember if I went to see any doctor about the head trauma. My car was totaled. The insurance got me into a brand new 1990 Toyota Celica STX, definitely the nicest car I had ever owned. I had just picked up my car when we got the orders to go to NTC (National Training Center) in the Mohave Desert, California.

Desert Storm

__NTC 1990__

My first thought when we got the orders to go to NTC, was why is a unit that has primarily trained for swamps and hills, training in the desert. Most troops specialize, and there were Bradley Battalions like ours in Texas that would have been doing all their training in the deserts. I believe somebody knew what was going to happen and was getting us ready. The only thing I couldn't figure out was why is it that something which sounded like it was a surprise event in the world later that year, was being planned for by our government before hand? Makes you stop and think though.

We closed down our buildings and vehicles in Ft. Stewart, GA and flew to Fort Erwin, California. There, we were issued Bradleys and trucks to train with. The training consisted of simulated battles with laser gear against a battalion of a mocked up versions of Soviet tanks, planes, and vehicles. Note: We fought against Soviet made vehicles in Iraq.

I had gotten my first Army Achievement metals as a Bradley driver over in Germany playing laser tag with Bradleys.

Desert Storm

It can be the wildest moving video game that you can imagine whether you are a driver or in the turret.

I'm just glad I didn't have to be the 11B (ground soldier) in the back. Imagine being bouncing around in a tin can in a severally confined space with six of your closest friends. There is no vented air and by the second or third day, everyone starts to smell ripe. By the end of the first week; well, you get the idea. There is no such thing as a hot shower every night in a war. Making sure you have clean sox is the most laundry you have time for. The 11B's had it the hardest. Spend each mission pulling most of the security when we stopped, ride in full combat gear for hours on end and then have to jump out under fire to secure the ground. Battles are only won when they have troops on the ground.

Since we got fewer trucks than we were used to working with, Top became the TC for Sean's truck and I spent the whole training riding in the back. I strung a hammock across the bed of the truck and read or slept most of the time. Top spent the whole time yelling at Sean. Towards one of the last days, Sean drove the truck into a big hill of sand to piss off Top who was in one of his moods. I got slammed against the front rack of the truck. I only got a few bruises. I really thought Top was going to hit Sean. That was the final straw for Sean and Top.

When we got back to Ft. Stewart, Top couldn't transfer him out of the company, but he did put him working for the company as the PLL (Prescribed Load List) clerk. The PLL clerk worked over at the Battalion building, ordering and keeping supplies for all the companies vehicles. Top figured he couldn't hurt himself or anybody else there. He didn't know then, but he had just put Sean right where he needed to be.

Over the 4th of July holiday, we got given two weeks of leave. Sean and I decided to drive out to the West Coast and visit our families and then drive back. Try out the new car. Sean didn't have a civilian driver's license, but I had been quizzing him on the driver's test questions for several weeks. Before we left, I took him down to the Georgia DMV and had him take the test. He couldn't believe I was actually going to make him take the test just before we left. Yes, he passed it the first time. It made it a lot easier to drive completely around this great country with an extra driver; I couldn't have done it by myself. We drove straight

Desert Storm

through from Georgia out I-10 west, all the way to Arizona and then cut across to Las Vegas and spent a couple of days.

When we left Vegas, I had as much money as I had left Georgia with from playing Blackjack. I had a cousin who used to be a dealer and had given me some advice for playing the game. The worst I have ever done is break even. Sean was down $400 from gambling alone, but on his last silver dollar, he won almost all of it back. I had to drag him out the door so he wouldn't go back and spend it. I didn't know he knew that many dirty words to call me. He did thank me later, but at the time, it was all I could do to get him out of the building and into the car. He just knew he could win more and now he had the money to do it.

From there we went to the San Francisco area. Sean and I visited with his brother and I spent time with some friends in Auburn. We went from there to his family's place in Portland and then to Idaho to visit my family. On our way back to Georgia, we stopped in Lacrosse, Wisconsin to visit a girl I had met on a trip over in Europe named Tammy.

I warned Sean to stay away from her 14 year old sister Darla. Just because Darla looked like she was 21, did not mean

Desert Storm

she really was of age. When we got there, Tammy and I went to the kitchen to get us some drinks; Darla offered to show Sean the pool room. We found her on top of Sean, kissing him on the pool table. He said she attacked him. The girls had grown up in an all girl Catholic school and could get a little wild. I tried to warn him. Tammy being the oldest was the only real reserved one of the 8 kids.

The next day, we were at a hypnotist show down town and Darla got chosen to be hypnotized. Before the hypnotist let her go afterwards, he put a suggestion in her head that whenever he said a certain word through the rest of his show, she would jump into the guys lap nearest her and scream "Sock it to me baby." The hypnotist did it three times before the end of his show. Tammy made sure I was well away from Darla, which put her next to Sean. Sean enjoyed that way too much. I kind of felt sorry for Sean, he was probably mentally about the same age as her at the time, and the first real pretty girl who ever paid any attention to him. She could have easily been a super model. It was all he could do to control himself. He sure did have that Banty Rooster strut going the whole weekend though.

Desert Storm

After our whirlwind tour of the country, Sean met a girl in Brunswick, GA named Betty and she introduced me to a friend of hers named Mary. Mary and I hit it off right away. We spent every moment together until we found out about my being deployed to Saudi Arabia for Desert Shield. I really liked this girl a lot, and she really seemed to like me too. Even though we were supposed to be on lock down, Sean and I would sneak down to see the girls whenever we got time, almost to the day we left. Because Mary's car was broken down, I left my new sports car with her when we left. That way I didn't have to have someone from home come all the way across the country to get it or pay big bucks to have it stored.

At first, I didn't believe that we would actually go. I had done lock down events in Germany. Stay on alert and ready to go until they have us stand down and go back to SOP (Standard Operating Procedure). I only had six more months left in my contract and wanted to switch jobs. I had only gone into infantry because it was all I could get being prior military when I joined the Army. I had to do the one tour as Infantry and then I could

Desert Storm

choose whatever job I wanted. I wanted something to take me through to retirement and not get me killed.

Desert Storm

Desert Shield 1990

In early August 1990, Iraq invaded Kuwait. Saudi Arabia, who is our ally and neighbor of Iraq, felt that they would be next. They asked us for help and gave us permission to bring military forces on to their soil for the first time in history. Our battalion was part of the Rapid Deployment Force and was instantly put on alert. Right away, we loaded our vehicles and supplies on to ships and sent them towards Saudi Arabia.

I have never had so many shots in my life. I felt like a pin cushion. I still wonder if there is a record that I could get a hold of, of all the shots they gave us. I have heard that some were just experimental. I also have heard that some records were lost. How convenient. Our country is well known for experimenting on its soldiers and then saying they are sorry when they get caught and blaming the soldier for being the problem. I love my country, but our government scares me. I have seen and felt what atrocities they are capable of. I hear all the time, politicians and big business men who say that if the average citizens knew what their

Desert Storm

government was really like, every one of the politicians would be hung for treason. Does anyone hear or care in America anymore?

We flew out on civilian airlines on the 24th of August 1990. That date will stay in my mind until I die. I think it was right after we took off from our fueling stop in Maine, that it started hitting everyone that this was real and that we really could be going off to war. As the Armorer, I was seated near the front because of all the small arms ammunition that we were bringing. The pilots had to figure extra weight on the flight because of the crates of ammo and the pilots and I had to balance it across the plane. Being the Armorer, I was in charge of security. Officer country was in first-class just ahead of me and the ammo.

The flight attendants were all volunteers and were really nice. I spent time drawing one of the pretty flight attendants. I was always very nervous about other people seeing my drawings, so I was keeping it down when she went by. One of the other attendants came up from behind and saw what I was doing, and called over the attendant that I had been drawing, to show her. He said he could tell right away who it was of and told me I had good taste. She was very flattered. I gave her the drawing and she gave me a kiss on the cheek and her phone number to call when I got home. Opportunities missed. I had several guys ask me to teach them how to draw to get girl's attention. Many of them had been hitting on her the whole flight and couldn't believe that she would go for me over them.

As we neared Ireland for our next fuel stop, Top came over to tell me that I would be in charge of setting up a perimeter around the plane when while we were being refueled and changing flight crew. Ireland could have possible terrorists. We were flying in a civilian Airline so no one should know who we were, but you never know. As we were rolling to a parking position, I issued ammunition to four soldiers plus myself. When they pushed the stairs up, each of the soldiers went to a tire and one stayed at the bottom of the stairs, all watching for possible snipers. I had to stand right in the door to see everything since I was sergeant-of-the-guards. I felt like a target. Everything went smooth though. The new flight crew were all volunteers since we didn't know what we were getting into too.

As the soldiers re-boarded, I had them turn back in their ammo and cleared their weapons. Right after take-off, the

Desert Storm

command announced that they had not heard from the 82nd airborne who was supposed to secure the airfield for us to set down in Dammam, Saudi Arabia. As we got closer, we still had not heard from the 82nd. People started to get real nervous when I was told to distribute crates of ammo down the aisles. They were saying we didn't have enough fuel to go anywhere else and that we might have to fight our way off the plane.

Until that moment, I didn't realize we had so many religious people on board. There was a lot of praying going on. Some people I would not have expected. This was the beginning of my journey of discovery into real human nature. I don't think you really know someone until you go through life threatening events together. Then, we see to what extent some people will go to survive. Some were what I called Crisis Christians. Back at home they were making fun of the religious people and now they were on their knees promising God all kinds of things, that I knew they would never follow through with, if God would only let them live through this. The anticipation of something was much more in my mind than fear. I guess that came from me always believing that whatever is going to happen, is going to happen whether I like it

Desert Storm

or not. Looking back, I felt like I was seeing things from a third person point of view.

We landed in Saudi Arabia with no problem. The 82nd was there, but no one ever told us what happened with the communications. After the comfortable cabin temperature of the plane, the heat was overwhelming. We were all in full combat gear. It was like putting a hair dryer on high and pointing it into your face. My eye watered and my throat and lungs felt like they were on fire. The pilot said it was 127 degrees Fahrenheit at the airport in Dammam. It felt like walking into an oven. It drained out every bit of energy I had. Each movement and breath was a struggle. If we had had to fight our way off the plane, we would have been in real trouble.

We were transferred by the Saudi's with trucks to some piers on the Persian Gulf which gave us a little relief. There was a nice breeze blowing in off the water which helped a little. This would be where we would pick up our vehicles which were shipped out two weeks before we flew out. We were to acclimatize for a few days and then start setting up a tent city for the people coming behind us. All we could do is eat, shit and sleep for the

Desert Storm

first few days. The Saudi government was supplying everything for us until our supplies arrived. The outhouses they gave us were swarming with crabs. I stood on the seat and squatted over the hole to use it. I was not going to set down. Several people caught them. Heat and scratching did not make for good tempers. No fists were thrown; that would have been too much effort, but it was better just not to talk to each other. They also fed us mango bread, mango juice, and other varied mango products for each meal. To me, mangoes are almost too sweet anyway and when combined with the heat, it was nauseating. I still can't look a mango in the face to this day. I was actually glad when we got MRE's. That didn't last long though.

Desert Storm

Sean and I trying to stay cool.

When our equipment arrived, I heard they added one extra Bradley to each company. The XO (Executive Officer, is 2nd in command of the company) would get it. I was assigned to ride with Sean again when we headed out to the desert once all our stuff was unloaded. Sean had his own 5 ton truck and trailer for all his vehicle parts he was to bring. Once we left the city, it was sand for as far as you could see. We stayed on a paved road for most of the first day headed west. With a poncho on top of the cab, we had some shade, but the heat coming off the engine didn't help. I picked up a bottle of water off the floorboard, where I had put it, and my fingers went right through the plastic. Water went everywhere. We learned real quickly to put our bottle of drinking water in a sock and then keep the sock wet to keep the water cool enough to drink. From that point on, improvising became a way of life. The militaries motto: improvise, adapt, and overcome.

When we headed out into the desert that evening, I was pulled into the gunner's position on the XO's new Bradley. I knew it hurt Top to do it, but they had no one else that was a sergeant and an 11M (Mechanized). 11M were the Bradley operating crew; everyone else in the company was 11B. (11B means front line ground troops) Not that I had gotten to do any of the training that everyone else had gotten to do prior to deployment. It did make it easier that the gunner's controls were just like a video game that I had played before. It makes me wonder if certain ways of making controls are just ergonomic or if someone designed it to take advantage of training we already have.

I moved all my stuff into the Bradley. It didn't have any of the seats for the dismount soldiers, so my stuff fit well. We also took on the NBC (Nuclear, Biological, and Chemical) sergeant. "Sergeant Wally Waters from Florida, at your service." Wally

Desert Storm

Waters was an odd person, but we all seemed to get along together well. Our driver was Dennis Chester. The only ones, who ever called him by his first name, were the XO and I; everyone else called him Chester. He was a real nice kid from Arizona; eager to please. He turned out to be one of the best drivers in the company. The XO was from North Carolina. He was the only one in our company command that didn't have a chip on his shoulder. As long as we talked straight to him, he treated us good. We just called him LT; short for Lieutenant. That turned out to be our whole crew for the war.

It showed real quick that military wheeled vehicles were not made for the desert. Hemtt trucks, which are the military version of the big semi truck, buried themselves right away. One driver kept his foot on the gas thinking he could pull himself out and the front end started to jump up and down. He got his front teeth knocked out by the steering wheel. Five Ton trucks did ok if they stayed away from the dunes, and Hummers could get around anywhere as long as the front end held together. A hard hit in the front end sheared off a simple cotter pin in the steering and the wheels would go whatever way the sand carried them. A simple

Desert Storm

sheared cotter pin in the steering could take out a whole vehicle and it happened quite often; bad design. That was Top's new ride for the war. After the first time it happened to ours, Sean kept several of the parts in stock. That had Top scratching his head because no one else in the Battalion could get any? Sean was starting to show his real gift.

The next three and a half months were a test in survival. We moved every few days or even every day. We were being told to not sleep in or on the vehicles, and to not sleep on the ground. Oh yeah, sorry, no cots either. What did they expect us to do, hover in the air? That's government thinking at work. We learned along the way which orders to listen to and which to ignore. We also had no running water; everything came from liter and a half bottles. We had MRE's for three meals a day. One of the medics had some Cajun seasoning that could even make MRE's tolerable. He got his dad to send over a case. I made sure I had one. I think after a couple months, we did get one cooked meal a week and a Friday night movie from the chaplain and his trusty generator.

We did all our laundry in cardboard boxes with garbage liners in them; one for wash and one for rinse. It only took ten

Desert Storm

minutes to fully air dry. You and your battle buddy worked together for showers and laundry. Sharing water rations was the only way to have enough to wash and drink. To shower, we stood on a piece of cardboard so you were out of the sand, next your buddy poured water over you so you could soap up. Then, he pours another so you can rinse off; then it is the buddy's turn. No modesty allowed.

Going to the bathroom became interesting. Peeing wasn't bad, but we were trained to dig holes for the other process, but the Dung Beetles would have it up the side of the hole and headed out into the desert before you could get done wiping. They would take the toilet paper too when you were done with it please. Why dig a hole, just get out of sight of everyone and don't slow the Dung Beetles down with the hole. Everyone gets what they want.

For sleeping and for many other things, we found that our ponchos were our life savers. For sleeping, we would lay them right in the sand. It was much more comfortable than the hard metal and could be molded for comfort. The plastic covered ponchos would draw moisture up underneath them and would draw the scorpions and the snakes under there instead of up with you for your moisture. Just be careful picking it up in the morning. Flip over an edge with your foot before you grab it and then watch the critters scatter when you pick it up. Shake well before putting it away. Don't leave your duffle bag open on the ground. No telling what could find its way in to set up housekeeping.

Before we found out about using our ponchos to sleep, one of the guys woke up one of the first mornings with something on his chest. He was freaking out and afraid to move. I unzipped his sleeping bag very carefully and pulled it back to find a big black scorpion sitting square in the middle of his chest. He didn't get stung, but it was a great way to get his blood circulating in the morning. Finding better ways of sleeping became a priority. It is hard to sleep when you may wake up with unwanted attention. No Stress here.

We would have to close the Bradley's up tight during sand storms. It was the only way to keep sand from getting into everything. The storms started off coming every Friday from sun up to sun down. It stayed as regular as clock work for a couple of months. As fall came in, it changed and wasn't as regular. We

Desert Storm

couldn't open hatches to trade radio duty during storms, so only one person would volunteer to do it for the whole storm. Getting sand into critical components could cost us our lives. Being on the XO's Bradley, we had to monitor radios 24/7. Imagine, being stuck inside a hot, stuffy metal box all day; it is brutal. We did get to get into the back which was a little cooler than the turret. There is a door between the main body and the turret which can be opened when the turret is turned forward and not operating. In the back, we could douse ourselves with bottles of water to stay halfway cool without frying electronics.

Outside is only slightly better. The poncho also worked great for sand storms. I would grab a box of water, MRE's for the day, and a good book. Make sure to pee before sun-up, tie the neck string of my poncho as tight shut as possible so sand couldn't get through, find a comfortable seat on the leeward and shady side and throw my poncho over myself and things to sit it out for the day. It got real hot, but there was a little air flow and, besides a little dust that got through, it was survivable. I kept a watered scarf over my mouth and nose to help me keep cool and to filter the air. I had to clean it now and then or it would clog with sand.

Desert Storm

Sundown would come, and the wind would stop. All you can do is shake everything out, look at the most incredible orange sunset that goes on forever in either direction, and thank whatever God you have, that you made it through another one. We endured through the pain and were rewarded with a view that has almost no description. The varying colors were like nothing else I had ever seen, and seemed to pulse.

The flies were terrible. Sand storms gave us the only relief from them. They would fly into your ears, eyes or your mouth at any and all times. Now I know what cows deal with. Breathing flies is nasty. They gave us some stuff to control the flies, which really didn't help much. It was granules of something, that when sprinkled with water, attracted the flies. They would then taste it and flip on their backs and spasm till they died. We called it fly agent orange. There were really too many of them for it to help much. It was mostly just entertaining to watch the death throes of the flies.

The nights were incredible. It would cool enough for the flies to disappear and the stars would come out. With no lights anywhere near on a moonless night, the Milky Way was a solid

Desert Storm

line of light from horizon to horizon. An hour after sunset till an hour before sunrise, the stars would be bright enough to see by. When the moon was out, it was just like a cooler daytime. You could see forever across the terrain; however, that was when the desert came alive; every creepy crawly out there started to move.

Most of the time between reading, I played spades with the guys. It was our only real outlet for time. It was too hot to train, so we just hung out for days. Every evening we would all gather around the radio and listen to Baghdad Betty, Desert Shield's version of "Tokyo Rose" from World War II. She always kind of scared us and also could give us a good chuckle. She would give our exact position out on the open radio (to the foot) every time she came on, even if we had just moved. She also told us we needed to go home because our wives were at home having sex with Tom Selleck and Bart Simpson. I still chuckle over that one.

Almost every day, we would see a small pickup truck in the distance that would stop and seemed to be watching us. It must have been who was telling Baghdad Betty our position. We were not allowed to pursue. It is kind of unnerving to be watched and followed with the chance of being attacked at any time. This was

Desert Storm

our day to day state of mind; staying alive. If the desert didn't kill you, the enemy might. The enemy could be over that next dune, and we would never have known it. You know what they say about military intelligence. There were very few fly-bys before the war, and that meant that the military must have been using satellites to keep watch over us. Sorry, but that didn't make me feel safe.

I spent every day, all day on duty. Besides being the only one with authorization for the ammo, the only other Sergeant who was infantry in Headquarters (HQ) platoon, was Staff Sergeant (SSG) Weston who was the gunner for the CO. He spent the first few months recovering from alcoholism. He was pretty much useless. DT's can get rough and he knew we were short handed, so he powered through. Everybody covered for him though. He was a nice enough guy and I had to respect that even though it was his own doing, he didn't whine. He sucked it up and kept moving. He did help me a lot later when I found things that I needed to know to fight as the gunner. The other sergeant we had in HQ platoon was Supply Sergeant Barons. His job was to do most of the running between our company and Battalion. He kept the food and water coming. He knew nothing about infantry, other than what he learned in basic. I was called the assistant platoon sergeant, but did most of the work.

Each platoon did get an authentic 8' X 8' Saudi Arabian Bedouin tent without the heavy wool inner liner which is the thing which helps cool you and keeps the dust out. It was good for shade for the daily card game and my office. Top, the CO, and the XO had a military tent (general purpose small) to themselves and stayed in there unless they needed something from us. We got good at setting them up and tearing them down.

We were getting mail from friends and spouses telling us what they were showing on the news, the nice air-conditioned housing we were staying at and that Egyptian whores were flown in to do our laundry. Where was our barracks, where were our Egyptian laundry ladies? They sure weren't going to let any cameras or news men near us. The general public would have been outraged at the conditions we lived in every day.

The local currency was cigarettes, Walkman batteries, real food and porn. Even though people were told not to send cigarettes by mail because of Saudi taxes, every couple of weeks,

Desert Storm

my girlfriend Mary would empty out a Little Debbie's cookie box and a carton of Camels would slide right in. She would then reseal it and you couldn't tell. Our mail ran so bad that sometimes I wouldn't hear from her for several weeks and then three would come in at once. I would be the cigarette god for a while. Sometimes I would get her letters out of order. It made for hard answering. You have to appreciate a woman who will break the law to make sure you are comfortable.

Whenever I saw Sean, who was with the Battalion headquarters, I would hand him cigarettes and he would hand me boxes of Walkman batteries. He was getting to be quite the "Radar O'Riley" (TV show M*A*S*H) in the supply position. If you needed anything, just ask Sean. He always seemed to know somebody, who knew somebody, who knew somebody, who could get what he wanted. Just ask.

Sean even ended up with a passenger for a while; a little black sheep. He said he got it from helping one of the local Bedouin. It didn't last long; he said he gave it away for its own good. We weren't allowed to eat local meats, so that was out. I think he got rid of it because of the comments from the guys about his new girlfriend. It did make for a good joke. You could see its little black head sticking out from under the canopy on the trailer when they were moving. I think it helped him to have a pet to talk to.

My grandmother and mother got together and sent me a half a case of *Nallies Chili* which must have cost an arm and a leg for the post. I very much appreciated it. I was a rich man. Peel off the label, throw a can of chilly out into the sand in the morning and it would be steaming hot by lunch. I made sure Sean got a couple cans. I only sold one, and that was for a couple more sticks of C4 explosives. I thought I got a great deal. They came in handy later.

We had one attempted suicide in our company. The wife of one of the guy's sent him a Dear John letter. We never found out where he got the ammo from. It took a little bit to talk him down and clear his rifle. All I could think was, that must be one low-life person to dump someone by mail when that other person may never come home again. He got shipped out that evening and we didn't see him again until we got home. We found out later that he

Desert Storm

was sent to a ship in the Persian Gulf for a psychiatric evaluation before they sent him home.

The command did come one time and load almost everyone into trucks and take them to a resort owned by a civilian oil company for one day of rest and relaxation. I didn't get to go. I was scheduled to run a range for shooting practice, which never happened. I ended up being the sergeant of the guards for those who were left to watch the Bradleys. I heard it was nice; swimming, pool tables, and junk food. I was not the happiest camper. I knew Top left me behind, just to piss me off. That is the kind of person he was if you got on his bad side. He had the power to make your life a living hell.

In mid December, we got put on division ammo guard duty for two weeks. They had showers, tents, cots, and cooked food. We felt like we had died and gone to heaven. Christmas brought mail for "any soldier" from the States. Besides our own mail, we usually got one or two boxes that were sent to "any soldier." I sent a thank you to everyone I got a package from, so they knew that it had made it and how much everyone appreciated those tokens. American people rock when they feel the cause. I also answered

Desert Storm

the regular letters from an Elementary school class that adopted me back home. There is no way for me to express how deeply all the letters and care packages meant to all of us. It can feel awful lonely for months on end in the desert feeling like you are forgotten by your government. We got a sand storm for Christmas. Christmas dinner was good if you didn't mind the grit in your teeth.

In the wadies.

Our company and Charley company got cross attached to 4/64 Armored Battalion after our stint on the guard duty. They were to be the spearhead of the invasion. That meant our battalion traded two Bradley companies for two M-1 tank

Desert Storm

companies. We were to be the boots on the ground during the spear head of the invasion. The whole tank battalion was hiding in some wadies, where we stayed until the air war started. Wadies are washed out ravines in some of the higher plateau areas. We also finally got our own outhouses, showers, tents, cots and two hot meals a day. Cold showers in a desert winter are still a brisk experience, and still doing laundry in a cardboard box was a pain in the butt, but it was better than what we had had up till then.

Life was interesting for a little while, or at least we just made it interesting. Right after moving to the wadies, The CO got the bright idea to have PT (Physical Training). Running, pushups, setups, and sand made it into a onetime deal. We had to entertain ourselves or go crazy, which I was already starting to wonder about.

SSG Weston and I started a rock garden. We found some small pebbles that had very unique markings and put them in rows outside our tent. Every morning and every evening, we would go out and water our garden. What everyone else didn't know was that SSG Weston and I searched around all during our day and would find rocks similar and just slightly larger than the

Desert Storm

ones we had started with. We would then switch them out on our guard duty each night. Over weeks, the rocks really were giving people the impression of them growing. Even if there was some marking on the rock that was a little different than the one we replaced it with, people would swear it was the same rock only bigger. It is strange how our minds can deceive us. Even Top was watching it and would just shake his head and walk away. I made the mistake to say something to him about it one day and he put me on shit burning duty at the outhouse. Sorry I commented. Usually only privates burned shit. It is a nasty job. Pull the half of a barrel that was being used, out from under the seat and pour gas and diesel into it, set it on fire, and then stir till it is all burned up. What a fun job.

Alcohol is strictly forbidden in Saudi Arabia. Several guys got some low grade wine out of grape juice and yeast, buried in the desert. They could do that now that we were setting for a while. It was nothing to party on. SSG Weston got to ride into a town close by one day. He came back with a case of near beer. He spent the evening drinking the whole case. He did offer me one, but if anyone else came up, he would growl and they would move

Desert Storm

away slowly and not make any sudden moves. When he finally finished the last one, I ask how he felt. He just said "full" and went to bed.

I had an entertaining show one day. Dennis actually caught and killed a sand viper. Sand vipers are very deadly and can bury themselves in sand very fast. He worked it into a rocky area where it couldn't hide, with his shovel, to finally catch it. He spent the rest of the day gutting it and scraping the hide. He then rubbed salt into it and staked it out on a board he found. After a couple of days of baking in the sun, it was hard as a rock. He lovingly worked it soft with flower scented hand lotion; it was all he could find. It made a beautiful hat band. However, I do not recommend catching or even messing with sand vipers. It could be a quick way to die. They call it a three step snake; three steps and you fall over dead if it bites you.

The board Dennis had found to stake his viper to, turned into a short hobby of sand boarding for us. I told you, we had to entertain ourselves. I screwed a couple of cloth scraps on to hold my feet and off I went.

Desert Storm

The medics received another shot for us! This one was delivered in a cooler. Yah, a cold needles in the butt cheek. I had heard about these before and the medics confirmed it, that you had to work it out of the muscle as quickly as possible or suffer later. I got mine, stepped back and started doing deep knee bends. It had gone in feeling very cold and feeling like someone had injected a golf ball in my butt. I just gritted my teeth and went for it. It hurt like hell. Wally Waters asked how I could withstand the pain. The rest of them were on the ground whining about how it hurt just to move. I guess I could think of it like "No Pain, No Gain." I am not sure that the gain of not being sore later was worth the cost of listening to everyone else whine and try to get out of duty for the next two days though. They should have listened and worked it into their system right away.

Charming the cobra was a fun event to watch from a safe distance. Several privates and Wally Waters had a lone cobra cornered in a rock ravine. They were taking turns getting in with a stick to make it dance. After watching the circus from a distance for a moment, a thought came back from orientation on local wild life. "Hey guys, where's its mate?" Cobras will have one of the

Desert Storm

pair be the bait while the other sneaks behind for an easy kill. There was a moment's hesitation and then each one trying to get out of the ravine as quickly as possible without getting near any big rocks. It was like watching the old Three Stooges movies. That goes into one of my all time favorite memory boxes. It felt good to laugh.

Our short term home.

To make myself feel safer, and because I was probably the only one who would, I liked to check the perimeter guards. Since I grew up hunting, individual stealth has always been one of my strong points. As sergeant of the guards, it was my job to issue ammunition, keep track of who was on guard, where, and check

Desert Storm

on them once in a while. I decided to also test our security. The first position I came on, one person was awake and the other was asleep. The sleeping guard wet his pants when I slid the back of my bayonet against his throat. After a few nights of catching guards sleeping, they got the point how vulnerable they were. The officers thought it was great, but the guys hated me. I felt safer at night though. Americans can get lazy real quick if you don't stay on us. They would never know when or where I would strike.

One night I was headed out to check the perimeter when I saw the light of a Hummer out in the desert, headed for our wadies. I headed for the guard's station that would intercept them as they got closer. It was about ten at night and we had just switched codes for the day. When someone comes into your perimeter, you are to stop them, give them the day's challenge word and they will answer with the day's response word. Which was what was happening as I came up on the passenger's side of the Hummer. Our guards had seen me and I signaled them to proceed. The answer for the day's code came back wrong. That was yesterday's code. Instantly I moved to the passenger door and found there to only be the driver and a passenger. Apparently,

Desert Storm

they had not seen me. They were focused on the two guards at the driver's door. The guards gave the challenge word again. When the vehicles driver gave the wrong response for the second time, I jerked the passenger door open, grabbed the passenger, threw him to the sand, subdued him and checked for weapons. He had a 45 pistol that he hadn't even gotten a hand on before I had him down on the ground and a knee to the back of his neck. I then checked him for ID. I had my knee in the back of his neck so he couldn't get up. The picture on his ID card was him; he was a Full Bird Colonel, from our side. I got off his neck, helped him to his feet as he was screaming at me and spitting sand. I then saluted him and handed back his side arm and ID, attesting to his identity. I saw that my troops had the driver against the other side in spread position. As we drove up to the CO'S tent, the Colonel promised me he would have my sergeant's stripes. After he left, I was called into the CO's tent. I figured I was going to get a court martial even though I had followed all the regulations. He and Top took one look at me and busted up laughing. They assured me that I had done everything by the book and that it couldn't have happened to a nicer person. I had to admit though, I did

Desert Storm

enjoy it. Using some of that training felt good. Take your time, breathe, and follow your training. It is amazing how quick word got around, not only in our company, but through the whole Battalion. I turned from the ass-hole sergeant to the enlisted men's hero. It was nice having my mail brought to me, and an extra chicken breast for dinner. How we all hungered for something to happen, just to break the monotony of our everyday existence. Everyone wanted to get to fighting or go home. The months of anticipation was wearing us all thin.

Desert Storm

Air War 1991

We watched the bombers go over the night the air war started. Just as they passed over us, they switched off their running lights to not be seen by the enemy. It was kind of creepy. It seemed like thousands of noisy fire flies just blinking out of sight and still feeling their sound vibrating through your bones. We wished them well.

The next day we were ordered to burn our showers and outhouses so they could not be later used against us. A truck took all our tents and cots away and we moved to a rally point to get us ready to be moved into our attack position.

I heard one of the other companies on the radio talking about one of their soldiers getting severely injured burning down one of the outhouses. When the whole story came out later, we found out it was someone going for the Darwin Award. Wikipedia defines The Darwin Award as: "…a tongue-in-cheek honor, originating in Usenet newsgroup discussions circa 1985. They recognize individuals who have supposedly contributed to human evolution by self-selecting themselves out of the gene pool via

Desert Storm

death or sterilization by their own actions." He had poured diesel on the outhouse and couldn't get it to do more than smolder, so he went and got a can of gasoline and crawled up on top of the smoldering outhouse to dump the gas over the top. He got burned over a large portion of his body and had to be medevaced out by helicopter. I never did find out how he eventually was, but I did hear when we got home that he had gotten a Purple Heart. What would you tell your family? "Grandpa, how did you get injured in the war?" "Oh, I was a moron." Now the U.S. people are paying his way till he dies, but real veterans who did their jobs have to struggle to get by or prove that they were injured. Not all injuries show on the outside. It feels to me like they devalued soldiers who got the Purple Heart by giving this moron any recognition. He is probably telling some big whopper of a story about what happened.

Desert Storm

Supply train headed for the invasion jump off point.

Everyone was keyed up. We had been in the Saudi Arabian desert for five and a half months and just wanted to do our job and go home. At the rally point, we had several chemical perimeter alarms go off. Instantly, everyone went into full chemical gear. The first time it happened, I was sergeant of the guards and it was about one o'clock in the morning. After several hand tests, our NBC sergeant, Wally Waters performed, showed negative, procedures say to have the lowest ranking person to crack their mask, take a breath, and then reseal their mask. Then you monitor them for ten minutes, and repeat once more before giving the all clear to the whole company. This is SOP (Standard

Desert Storm

Operating Procedure). Risk one to save the many. I had someone get the new kid who had just gotten there just a couple weeks ago. He looked to be about 17 years old and fresh out of boot camp. I told him what he was to do and he told me flat out "NO." Top pulled my pistol out of my holster, cocked it, handed it to me and told me to repeat my order again. During war time in the military, refusing an order is punishable by instant death. No judge, no jury. BANG and move on. You get a carton of cigarettes and a transfer to a new unit. This sounds harsh, but to keep and hold respect of a group trained and primed to kill, I knew it was the only way to hold my command. Before I could repeat the order, Wally Waters pulled his mask off in disgust and threw it on the ground between us. This was him volunteering to stop what was about to happen. I cleared the chamber of the pistol and put it back in the holster. I still don't know to this day if I would have been able to pull the trigger. If I couldn't have done it, I could have been charged with disobedience and shot right there also. The young kid was transferred out of our company before sunrise. When I got by myself, my knees buckled. I just lay there and cried. Wally Waters defused the situation by being a

Desert Storm

volunteer and saved me from making a decision I am not sure I could have lived with. Reading that order as a regulation is one thing, but following through puts individual morals to the test.

View from the turret while being hauled on trucks.

After a couple of days of playing, how fast can you get into a full chemical gear from all the chemical alarms going off, and watching bombers heading north, they finally got all the vehicles loaded on to Saudi trucks and we headed North. We were headed to where we would be deployed from for the ground assault. Trucks could move us faster and not damage roads. The air

Desert Storm

strikes had knocked out all their communications and by moving then, they would not know where we would be striking from.

Hafar Al Batin was right at the T in the road where we turned west to paralleling the Iraqi border on Saudi Highway 85. Our truck was one of the last in the convoy. The LT had gone ahead in the advanced party, so it was just Dennis, Wally Waters and I in our Bradley being towed by a semi. Before we could get out of the city, I felt something give under us and the Saudi driver pulled over. Before the company got too far away, I radioed the CO to tell them we had axle problems on the truck we were on. They told us to set tight and they would send someone back for us. I had no idea that it would take them 2 days to get where they were going and another two days to get someone back to us.

The driver was an asshole and thought he had the right to tell me what to do. He wanted us to stay on the trailer. Against the driver's wishes and without unhooking our chains, we unloaded ourselves off the trailer. I had Dennis do a pivot steer which broke the chains and then he just drove off the side of the trailer. I felt like we were sitting duck with buildings on three sides and across the road, open desert. It would have been easy to attack us there,

Desert Storm

no matter what the truck driver wanted. A lone Bradley would have been a prime target. That trailer was not going anywhere for a while with a busted axle. Better safe than dead.

I fixed our security issue real quick. There had been an MP post set up at the T where the southerly road went out into the desert, so we pulled over there and told them our position. They seemed glad for us to be there. All they had were a couple of Hummers and machine guns. They told us that if we would park behind them and move the turret around a couple times a day, they would stand all our guard duty. They had to do it anyway. We just made them look bad ass with their own tank backing them up.

All of us took a turn getting some time away from the Bradley. I figure with at least two of us all the time to drive and shoot, it would be safe to let someone get out and away. Hafar Al Batin was an interesting town. The main East West road was the divider between the desert and the southern edge of the city. There was a public phone only one block from where we were, in a park. I ran up a hundred dollar a day phone bill calling collect back to the states. While waiting in the line for the phone, I got to

Desert Storm

talk to soldiers from almost all over the world. Most were from Europe and Saudi's neighbors. Even though there were some language barriers, everyone seemed to find a way to get their point across. The main subjects were food and women. Soldier will be soldier, no matter where they come from.

The first evening, Wally Waters came back from his time in the city with this chunk of stuff that looked like camel shit and said that the Saudi's were smoking it and he thought it was hash. He made a can pipe and tried to smoke it. It smelled like burning camel shit. I wasn't going to try it. Wally Waters said it just burned his throat and gave him a headache. The next morning, as I was doing my regular duties, I heard Wally Waters telling one of the MP'S about his "hash." All I could think was, great, he is going to get himself thrown in jail. To my surprise, the MP said he could get us some real hash if we had something good to trade. Later that day he was there with a chunk of brown hash about the size of a small base ball that he said he got from the Saudi MPs. He gave us the whole thing for half a stick of C4. I had not smoked any marijuana in years, and figured, hey, I am going off to possibly die, why not. That day, we realized we were getting

Desert Storm

low on water and food, so I traded the other half stick of C4 to some French soldiers for some of their meals. For the next couple days, we were living the good life again. The French have wine, sausage, cheese and those nice butter crackers in every meal. We need to learn from the French. MRE's are nasty, especially when it is day in and day out. We did also find a place that would give you half a chicken and a plate of rice for two American dollars. I had money; there had been no other place to spend it in the desert.

Desert Storm

Highway of Death before the ground war started.

It took us two days up the highway of death (Saudi Hwy 85) to get to our drop off position. There were crashed and burned out vehicles along both sides of the road all the way there. I was surprised we didn't get side swiped somewhere along the way, as close as we were getting to cars and trucks heading the other way. We found out later that most of the casualties of the war came from that road. We finished off the last of the hash the night before we got there. When we got to the drop off point, I could see no landmarks and only desert in every direction. The truck driver wasn't much help; he just pointed and said "20 kilometers that way." We headed in the direction that he pointed without any

Desert Storm

landmarks, no compass, maps or GPS or even tracks. There had been a sand storm recently. All I knew was 20 kilometers was a little more than 12 miles, without any way of tracking miles. I wasn't even sure the driver knew where to drop us off. I was getting real nervous about having gone too far when we finally sighted our tanks. We had come right up on our 4/64 Battalion HQ. They had someone come get us and lead us to the wadies our company was assigned. If you crawled to the top of the wadie we were in, you could see the sand burm that marked the border between Saudi Arabia and Iraq just to the north of us.

    The LT was happy to see us. We had most of his gear. Again, Wally Waters started running his mouth to the LT about our adventures, including the hash. The LT was not looking very happy. He called me off to the side and asked if we still had some. I told him it was all gone, thinking I was in for big trouble. Instead he says "Shit, you could at least have saved me a little" and warned me to shut Wally Waters up before he did get us into trouble. I told Wally Waters that if I heard that he had told anyone else, I would shoot him. He got the message.

Desert Storm

It was around this time that they started giving us what they said were nerve agent pills. Supposedly they were small amounts of nerve agent which was supposed to build up our immunity. We didn't find out until later that they had never been tested for long periods of time and had never been tested on a human. All we knew was that within 30 minutes of taking it, we had to defecate; everybody, and it was white. That is not right. We were told to take them once a day. We had to time our pills when combat started because it was the only way for everyone to stop and defecate at the same time and not have to stop more often and slow us down.

By this time, I was starting to lose track of days. I am still not sure how many days we spent there. The command vehicles (which included us) would go out at night and practice maneuvering and keeping our place within a wedge fighting formation with the rest of the battalion. Between those times, our soldiers did recon on foot into Iraq and our Bradley would be their radio contact. I would sleep whenever I got the chance.

One evening, just after dusk, we were as close to the border as possible to still see over the burm for direct line of sight

Desert Storm

communication with one of our patrols when we saw a fog or dusk bank moving in just to the North and East of us. Fog is almost non-existent here and dust means someone was moving because there was no wind, so this got our attention. Then we saw what looked like lights going back and forth from north to south and then from south to north within the dust. The XO and I decided to call battalion and have them send an airplane by to check it out, because the unit to our right didn't see what we were seeing at all. I am not sure how far they were away, but it should have been right between us and them. Within a couple of minutes, two jets came screaming by from east to west and then turned around and went by in the other direction. Just before they got there, the lights stopped. They reported seeing nothing either. The XO and I couldn't believe they weren't seeing anything because it was pretty obvious to us that something was going on. Battalion was not happy with us calling in what they called flawed reports. Then, early the next morning just before dawn, I started hearing gunfire going off near our wadie. I woke the LT and we crawled to the top of the wadie where we could smell gunpowder, but the shooting had stopped. While the LT and I were doing recon, the

Desert Storm

radio watch called the other platoons in our company and asks for a status report. Each one reported all clear. When we got back, the LT woke the CO and he called in another air recon. They went by again and reported nothing going on. By this time, Battalion was furious. Since I was the top enlisted who was part of both of those incidents, and low man on the totem pole, there was talk of having my head on a platter; I had gone over the edge. I never even got an apology when it came out the next day that one of the platoons had had an ammo can go off from being too close to the heater which they weren't suppose to be running. The lieutenant of that platoon hadn't said anything because it was his Bradley and his orders to let it run. I had started to think I was going crazy. I was so angry, that I was thinking, thanks for covering your own asses. After spending a year and a half with this company and with all the things we had been through, you would think that I would feel that bond you always hear about with soldiers. It wasn't there, and I had to go into combat with them.

    We had to put orange flags on the back of each Bradley turret so that our planes could tell enemy from friends. During

Desert Storm

our last minute training, it was found that pilots were miss identifying targets.

Somewhere in this time period, I was called into the CO, so he could inform me of the good news that I had been involuntarily extended in my term of service for another six months. I was supposed to be getting out on March 1st. My birthday was March 3rd. I got to spend it in combat.

Desert Storm

Last minute checks and instructions.

Ground War (Desert Storm)

I think it was a late afternoon when the bulldozers knocked down a hole in the burm for us to start our assault into Iraq. Time doesn't seem to be in order in my head. I will try to lay it out in order as best that I can remember. I had been up since early that morning doing last minute checks. We knew the ground assault was close, but didn't know exactly when.

Rolling on the battle field is so much different than training, not that I had gotten much of that until the last few days before

Desert Storm

the war. When you are worried about being shot at, keeping up speed and keeping position, the terrain comes at you much faster. We could not fall out of position by going around bad terrain. Even if it meant 20' drops and then climbing 20" back up all within less than a minute. Damn wadies! The gunner's job was to scan back and forth in his coverage area and assessing for threat. Coverage area is your particular direction to watch and area to defend. By overlapping yours with the Bradley who is covering on each side, we could cover 360°. My coverage area ended up being floater in the rear of the wedge shape we were running in. As a floater, I could move to any position that needed help. Since we were the XO's Bradley, we did most of the communication, and our gun could support any weak points in our formation. The CO's Bradley was dead center in the wedge so they could see everything that was going on. It didn't take very long at all for the gunners to have bruises all over their faces from having their faces slammed into the sight repeatedly at 40+ mph for days at a time. This was all cross country and wadies could appear out of nowhere. I would compare it to getting hit with gloves as opposed to getting hit bare fisted by a trained boxer. Because the turret

Desert Storm

was above the main body of the Bradley, we got thrown harder. It is literally dropping 10-40 feet hitting the bottom and then climbing the other side without slowing down. With the shock absorbers on a Bradley, a speed bump can really bounce you around. Some of the hits I took rattled me good. It is rough and loud inside a Bradley, especially in the turret. The M-1 Battle tanks on the other hand, had great shocks and were made to look like they floated across things at a lot higher speeds than we could go. We only took half the fuel the M-1's did though.

Me in the gunner's hatch.

Our first combat encounter pushed me to the edge. We were taking on small arms and shoulder fired rockets from a dug in

Desert Storm

position. I turned to take out an RPG rocket position. I pulled up on target and my 25mm fired once and locked. Instantly I had Dennis swing us into the middle of the wedge we were in, to take us out of the combat. I opened the access panel and found that one of the ammo feeder shoots had become disconnected. I knew right away that I was the one to blame for getting us all killed. It was a very terrifying event. I hadn't checked that latch to make sure it was completely locked. As it cycled a second round in, it popped off and jammed the whole belt. While still moving and under fire, I pulled it all apart and reset everything faster than I could ever believe possible; which is no easy affair when you are sitting still, let alone in the middle of combat. It usually takes about 15 minutes sitting still. Just as I was setting the receiver back in, the Bradley lurched forward and then backward really fast. I don't even know what we hit. The main gun receiver weighs about 40 pounds and your arms are reaching into a recess at arm's length with no extra room. I felt my right shoulder come out of the socket as it went forward and then it got slammed right back as the Bradley went the other way. The LT said he would have given me a medal because of how fast I did it while we were moving and

Desert Storm

in combat at the same time, if he had not known it was one of my SNAFU's (Situation Normal, All F**ked Up) in the first place. Adrenalin can help you do amazing things. By the time I got ready to do a test fire, we were already past the combatants. We moved out of the wedge and I took a couple shot to make sure it was going to work. That is not a good way to start combat. Even though my nerves were already shot and my shoulder hurt and was swollen, we still had days and miles to go before we could rest. I was not going to let my crew down again.

One day, we came up on six soldiers walking through the desert. Between them, they had two rifles, one pistol, ten rounds of rifle ammunition for the rifles, and none for the pistol, half a loaf of moldy bread and part of a canteen of dirty water. Only two of them had shoes which were so worn, they were falling off their feet. If we had not found them, they would have died soon. One of our soldiers had one of the Iraqi soldiers face down on the ground and was searching him for weapons. The guy kept turning and kissing his hand or his arm and saying "U.S. gooood, Saddam Bad," then spitting. Our soldier later said that the soldier couldn't have weighed over 70 or 80 pounds, which he found out when he

Desert Storm

picked him up after cuffing his hands together. They had been hurting for a while. We gave them each a bottle of water and an MRE while we guarded them; waiting for someone to pick them up by one of the rear units. The guy sitting near me opened one of the food packets, took a couple bites and started to close it back up. I finally figured out that he was still hungry, but thought that was all the food he was going to get and was trying to save it. I poured the rest of that case of MRE's into his lap. All of their eyes got big and they tore open what they had started and ate well. Later the interpreter was telling us they were sure it was going to be terrible being our prisoners, but it was better than dying slowly with Saddam's troops. They were told we were barbaric and couldn't understand kindness. They were pleasantly surprised. Other than fuel stops and nerve agent pill induced bathroom breaks, that became the longest stop we made.

From tidbits that I got from the LT and the CO talking and from translations I had done on coded messages, I realized that we had not been expected to live through the first few days and that there was no extra supply train behind us to keep us going. We were told that we had to make a run to Jalibah Airfield on

Desert Storm

what supplies the battalion had left, and secure the airfield so they could fly supplies directly to us there. If we didn't make it or we ran out, oh well. They had figured we were supposed to be dead anyway. We were all already running on no sleep and borrowed time since the ground war started.

I was put under orders to not share that information with anyone in the company. They didn't want people to start a panic and be seeing what their country's government thought of them. I heard later that they had expected 90 percent casualties. I realized I was just cannon fodder to them. It was hard for me to take knowing that you are a throw away play toy. Knowing that and other things I witnessed has colored my view of my wonderful government. We are taught to give our lives for our country, our friends, and family as a soldier, but needless sacrifice for protecting a country that would later be the home of most of the 9/11 terrorists, does not seem to fit with that concept for me; especially when I am the one giving my life. I believe that some of what the Iraqi soldiers said was true. If you just go by the actions of our government towards its people and people of other countries, they are barbaric and can't understand compassion;

Desert Storm

anything for the almighty dollar at everyone else's expense. Sorry, that soapbox slid right up under me.

The next resistance we met was really light. I noticed that several Bradleys were firing their big gun against small arms fire, which is against the Geneva Convention. You are not to use any weapon bigger than the weapon used against you. Cannons against small arms is wrong and is one of the first things that are taught in combat school. Not too far past the combatants, were some Bedouin tents. Even though nobody fired at us from there, several of the Bradleys started to fire into them with their cannons. A woman came running out holding what looked like a baby. Both she and whatever she was holding up was covered in blood. Immediately I said something to the LT about these being non-combatants and they needed to cease fire. I can listen to what is going on in the company, but from my seat, all I have is interior communication. The LT had to make the call, and by that time, we were already by. When I brought it up to the CO later, he told me to let it go, for my own good. I didn't say it to him, but it sounded like a threat the way he had said it. I did find out whose Bradleys those were and who the gunners were. It didn't surprise

Desert Storm

me to find out who it was pulling the trigger. Later, I heard one of them laughing about putting Rag Heads down while they were still young. The whole thing made me sick to my stomach. To me, it was just murder of innocent civilians.

The next time we stopped for fuel, they could only give us two minutes of fuel because we were so limited. That is whatever they can pump into your tank in through a two inch nozzle in two minutes. They were big hoses, but we were almost empty. That didn't give us much. But then, we were almost out of water, food, and ammunition also.

We on the XO's Bradley were using even more fuel and getting less sleep than everyone else. Not that anyone was getting much sleep. We were the ones running back and forth to the supply train on errands when everyone else was getting a short break. No rest for the wicked. By the time we made it to Jalibah, I was working on nearly four days of scanning almost nonstop and without sleep. When everyone got into position just short of the airfield just after dark, we were sent back to the supply trains to get one of our Bradley's which had broken down and been left for

Desert Storm

the supply train to pick them up. The supply train was just behind us.

As we were working our way to the supply train which was about 10k back, I noticed a heat signature just behind some dunes. I was using a thermal night sight which work purely off of heat. The thermal sights are much more sensitive than our daytime sights. If it was some kind of enemy sneaking up behind our company, we had to find out. As my sights cleared the dune but kept us still somewhat under cover, I saw that it was a Hemtt fuel truck stuck in the sand. As we approached, the Hemtt crew was freaking out pretty bad. They only had one set of night vision goggles, with which you can't see very far and were hearing a tracked vehicle coming at them through the dark in a combat zone. We found out, when we finally got them calmed down, that they were part of 1st battalion 7th Infantry, based out of Germany and had gotten separated from their supply train. They weren't sure where they were or even if they might have been behind enemy lines. We told them that if they topped us off, we would pull them out. They told me they couldn't do that, so I asked Dennis to act like he was going to pull away. Immediately they

Desert Storm

agreed to fill our tank but we had to pull them out and take them somewhere safe. We dropped them off at our Battalion when we picked up our other Bradley. It was nice having a full tank again.

When we got back to the company, the shelling had started to pound the airfield and soften them up before we rolled in. Intelligence was sketchy about what damage the bombers had done to the air field. They would send bombers in at night and then the next day would look at satellite images to assess the damage and hardly anything looked hit. Military Intelligence was scratching their heads, or maybe it was their balls. So, we were stuck not knowing if we were walking into a well dug in resistance or what.

The LT announced to our crew that we would have about two and a half hours before we moved again and went to the CO's Bradley. I told Wally Waters that I was sleeping and not to wake me. I didn't even get up from my seat; I set my alarm and just put my head down against the sights and was out. I remember hearing my alarm go off two hours later because it didn't match the sound of a Bradley moving in my dream. Even in my dreaming we were still moving and I was still scanning back and forth and back and

Desert Storm

forth. Gunners have tunnel vision through the sights. They can only see what is in front of them when they turn the turret. Coming back to being awake after so little sleep which seemed like no rest, I was still having tunnel vision and had problems negotiating back threw the Bradley from the turret and out the back hatch door. Peripheral vision is hard to take when you have been living on tunnel vision for days on end. I had been so out of it, I didn't even remember the LT coming back. I say hatch door because this is just a man door in a ramp that drops open in the rear of the Bradley to expose the whole inside. The Ramp is made for the soldiers to dismount very quickly under fire. This "hatch" was barely big enough for one small guy with no gear. Wally Waters was laughing at me the whole time. When I finally got my legs underneath me to steady myself, I looked up. There was a light fog down low this far north just before sunrise, and a few trees. The stars were out bright. I could see the Milky Way from horizon to horizon, and everything was dead quit. I thought I was still in some kind of dream. Wally Water's talking onto a recorder reminded me where I was. I still have a copy of that tape. I decided to take what time I had left to shave. I had very little

Desert Storm

water, but I also didn't want my protective mask to fail in battle because I had stubble keeping it from sealing. Besides, it would wake me up. After washing my face and lathering up, I started the first pull up my neck with the razor, when our artillery friends decided to get one more volley off before we rolled. They were behind us about half a mile or more and shelling over our heads. We could see the flash of the mortars, hear something come screaming over and then see the flash of the impact in front of us. It startled me so bad; I thought I had cut my own throat. Predawn artillery; that will wake you up.

Just as I was putting everything away, the five minute call to roll out came in. I could still hear the shelling from inside the turret. It was our cue to move when the shelling stopped. When we came out of the woods at the edge of the airfield, it was bright enough that we could have gone off of our thermal sights, but I decided to keep mine on. The whole assault force (Bradley's and M-1 battle tanks) were stretched out along the southern fence line as far down the airfield as I could see. We were at the hangers and runway end of the field. Once everyone seemed to be in one line along the fence, the order was given to open fire. We were to

Desert Storm

destroy anything that moved. I was watching one of the hangers when I noticed a lot of hot air coming out of vertical vents in the rear of the hanger. I just had time to get a couple shots off, as a plane came screaming out of the hanger. I saw my shells hit the tail section, leaving two yellow dots, as it started to climb away. Nothing is ever like the movies, there was no big explosion when I hit it, but as he climbed, I could see the yellow dots of flame getting bigger and then the pilot ejecting as the plane rolled over and crashed. Then there were explosions and flames. The LT started letting everyone know about the heat signature just before takeoff, while I started looking for another target. The Iraqi pilots were revving the engines to full throttle in the hangers and then releasing the brakes in order to take off straight out of the hanger. The jet wash was being diverted up and out the back of the hanger. One of our guys timed his shot so perfectly, that the plane came out of the hanger into three rounds. They didn't even get off the ground; it just skidded to a stop and exploded. Any dug in positions were just hammered by the force of our assault. It didn't take long before everything stopped moving. As we looked around, we saw that some of the hanger had tarps stretched over

Desert Storm

big holes in the top. The tarps were painted the same as the concrete. That was why Intelligence couldn't figure out what was happening, the tarps hid the damage. We saw big pipes lying across 55 gallon drums, which from satellite photos would look like a mortar position, and holes in the runways that had been filled with dirt and painted the color of asphalt. I had to laugh, they had fooled our guys; so much for Military Intelligence.

Because we were to be the troops on the ground, we were ordered to swing around to the western end of the airfield and sweep back east, through the middle of the airfield. As we approached the West end, we were to the left side of the formation and rear. As we were swinging a little wide, I saw some kind of heat signature out in the desert a little further west. The CO and LT discussed it and we went with two other of our Bradleys to check it out. What we found was a pit in the sand that was so big, that it was hiding several thousand staff and families. They must have been there for the last couple days, hiding from the shelling. I thought there was going to be a stampede; they were told we would kill everyone. We backed away and sent their position to

Desert Storm

the higher ups to deal with it and headed back to the company. I never did find out what happened to them.

When everyone was in position for the next attack, we started picking away at the bunkers until we weren't taking any more fire and then we started moving through the airbase; orders-destroy everything. For some reason, I don't have a lot of memories of the event. As I look back at it, it is a jumble of unconnected memories. I know a lot of people died. I do remember that about half way through the airfield, mortars started falling all around us. The LT called Battalion to have some airplanes find and take care of the mortar position. The call came back several minutes later saying it was our own mortars firing on us. It took a while for it to stop. We were so lucky none of them were a direct hit or it could have taken one of us out. One of the BC's in our company got shrapnel in his elbow because he was foolish enough to have his hatch open; supposedly to see better. He was lucky to not get it in his head.

One Bradley in Charley Company took a round through the back door; killing the driver and wounding two others. It was noted that it was a Bradley 25mm round that had done it. No one

Desert Storm

knew for sure who had pulled the trigger. It could have been any one of us that could have misidentified the target and pulled the trigger. For all I know, it could have been me and did not know what I had done. It is a sobering thought that can haunt you for years, even though I know I was not anywhere near to Charley Company when it happened. I know it is an irrational thought, but it still persists. Later, we were told that 80 percent of all the casualties were friendly fire; meaning, that we were our own worst enemy.

Desert Storm

Our crew, right after Jalibah Airfield.

My next full memory was lying on the back ramp smoking a cigarette, having our picture taken near the airfield and then a sniper shot hitting the Bradley right next to my head. Everyone sat there for a second; not realizing what it was until I yelled "sniper" and everyone tore back to their fighting position. One of the dismount troops from another Bradley picked off the sniper. Command decided it was not safe there, and we moved on towards an ammo depot that was supposed to be nearby; so much for getting some rest.

I remember being attacked soon after. As we were moving towards our next objective, it looked like open desert all around

Desert Storm

us until soldiers started popping up out of the sand. They had been hiding under blankets covered by sand. I remember an RPG round coming right at my sights and turning the turret and then I remember waking up in the back of the Bradley. I was not even sure how long I had been out; it could have been minutes, or it could have been hours, but the fight was already over. The RPG had hit us on a glancing shot and just left a burn mark on the turret. The concussion was what had knocked me out. I couldn't believe I was still alive. I must have been hurt more than I thought from the concussion of the round. From here, my memory gets worse. I don't remember getting to the ammo depot or fighting at all. My next memory is waking up and it was just getting light outside, and that we had taken the ammo depot. At least I had felt like I had had a long sleep and other than a splitting headache, I felt a little better.

That morning the CO said that he would be using our Bradley to take some news reporters into the middle of the ammo depot and do an interview. I was to stay in the back and make sure they couldn't look out to see where they were being taken. We had fun with the sound guy. This was his first time in a

Desert Storm

combat zone and the first time on a military vehicle. As he was sitting on a case of ammo, he asked if there was anything that was explosive back there. I told him about the box he was setting on and the C4 explosives above his head and he moved to the floor. The reporter and the camera man both were rolling with laughter. They were both combat veterans. I recognized the reporter, but I don't recall his name. As they were getting set up to interview our commanding officer, we fixed our morning coffee and breakfast. We had gotten a few rations, but not much. The sound guy started to freaked out again when he saw us using C4 to heat our coffee. C4 explosives need both heat and compression to explode. It puts off a lot of heat, just don't stomp it out after you're done. Morning coffee is important.

As we looked around at the ammo depot, we noticed that some of the ammo had Jordanian markings and the shipping dates were after we had gotten to Saudi Arabia. Jordan was supposed to be our ally. What were they doing supplying Iraq against us? That little bit of information never got out to the public. It is interesting how a lot of things didn't get out. I have heard people say that there is no way the government could hide secrets; that they are too dumb. Our government is good at misinformation. Some of the caches had biological weapons; weapons of mass destruction.

One cache in the ammo depot

We found out later, that this same ammo depot was blown up afterwards by our own soldiers; it was ordered by higher command. SOP (Standard Operating Procedure) says that you can blow up any ammunition, except biological weapons. They are to be burned. Blowing up biological weapons doesn't destroy them, it only scatters them. Even though our government knew

Desert Storm

that, they blew everything up anyway. Our company was not far away, down wind. I heard several years later, that anyone who was within a couple of miles of the explosion died soon after. Our government has now had more than 20 years to study what it has done to the rest of us. If it is like any other experiment, the general public won't find out the results until us and the people who were in charge, who gave the orders, are gone and buried. That way they protect the people who gave the orders. The government has taught me that it is easier to do first and ask for forgiveness later, than to ask for permission, because you wouldn't get it anyway.

We went from the ammo depot towards the Euphrates River to cut off access on the northern most highways, by all troops trying to retreat out of Kuwait back towards Baghdad. Our company came across some underground bunkers. No one fired at us, so everyone except the BC's and drivers were told to dismount and search the bunkers on foot. I couldn't believe when I was told to dismount with Wally Waters as my combat buddy. He was not trained for combat and had only been riding around in the back since we started. Guts and glory was all he could think

Desert Storm

about. I warned him to be quiet and keep his eyes open. There was a minefield all across the front with narrow sections open for access. It was all I could do to keep him out of the minefield just to get to the entrance into the section of bunkers that we were assigned to clear. After all my instructions to him, the dumb shit jumps down inside the entry to the tunnels, turns up the tunnel to the right, screams and starts running up a tunnel that I could only crouch in. I figured he wrote his own death warrant. But, Wally Waters is living proof that God looks out for fools and children. He never ran into anyone or anything worth coming across until he ran into our 3rd Platoon. They said he sounded like a freight train coming at them. They got him back across the minefield and back to the Bradley safely. I'm surprised he didn't shoot someone from 3rd platoon. Me, on the other hand, I turned left and was moving slowly, sweeping with my hands for possible mines. I came across two. They were simple to disarm, but hard on the nerves. The only reason I could come up with, for Wally Waters' not blowing himself up, was that my tunnel led to officer's territory and the Amory, his just went to the fighting positions. The Iraqi command wanted to protect themselves from their own soldiers as well as us.

The first room I passed was empty. It looked like it had been an office. At the next room I heard voices. I took a quick peek and saw two Iraqi soldiers who looked like they were clearing out a safe. Both of them were armed. I thought to myself, breath, and don't hesitate if need be. You're just doing your job. It is much harder fighting face to face, than fighting from the Bradley. In a Bradley, it is like playing a video game and you don't see the person eye to eye. When it is just you or them, it becomes personal. I would rather not go into any more details about this. I didn't have the time to think about what had just happened just then, I was still on the job and in danger. That gun fire could have called their friends. I went from there, on up the tunnel. No more mines. There were at least one or more people in the armory section, but they ducked out as I came in. I heard them but didn't see them. They had to have heard the shooting grab things and ran.

I was told by some of the intelligence guys, that many of the soldiers had been black-mailed into fighting. They were told

Desert Storm

"fight or have your family slowly killed off." Supposedly the proof was in that safe, at least for this unit. We found files on all the soldiers and their families. That was hard to take, knowing that they didn't want to fight any more than I did.

After I had confirmed that it was all clear, I tried to concentrate my attention on the Russian weapons in the armory instead of the fighting. I had seen most of the weapons before, but had never had a chance to inspect or fire them. I grabbed two AK-47 rifles from straight out of the box. One had the straight grip and the other had the drop grip. I also found two Berretta 9mm pistols, one serial number apart. It said licensed by Berretta on one side and had the local language on the other. The Ak-47's were great weapons to fire. I hung on to them for a while over there. They were much better weapons than our M-16's. By focusing on the weapons, I didn't have to see the faces in my head.

Desert Storm

Captured AK47's

After the all clear was called, the LT decided to come out of the Bradley and take a look around. He was half way across the minefield when I caught sight of him. It took us two hours to get him back out of the middle of the minefield. I still don't see how he didn't blow himself up. Getting across a mine field intentionally, takes patience and nerve. It requires finding and marking all the mines. One slip and you die. You can't just retrace your steps. You can just bump one that you didn't see and it could go off. As I was working to get him out, we were joking

Desert Storm

back and forth. He said his legs were cramping from staying still for so long. My nerves were shot. I will admit it, I had to find somewhere to sit and cry afterwards. No one said a word to me. It had been a long day.

The tragedy to the locals was very present in that area. One day, we were moving down the road and children were begging alongside the road. We were crossing through secured territory, standing up in the turret and last in our convoy. I could see several women back across a field in the tree line watching the children. As one Bradley threw out an MRE, a little girl grabbed it. She couldn't have been more than five or six years old. She had pretty little ringlets hanging down and the face of an angel. She looked so much like Mary's little daughter Susan. I couldn't believe when a bigger boy came over, punched her in the face and took her MRE. I heard Dennis say "Holy Shit, did you see that!" I told him to get us in between that little girl and the rest of the kids. She started walking back towards the tree line holding her nose. The LT told him to stay on the road. Dennis didn't listen to the LT and swerved off between the girl and the others. The LT dropped back down through the hatch. I was keeping my hand on

Desert Storm

the trigger and turret controls in case of trouble and wondered what the LT was up to. As we pulled alongside the little girl, the LT came buck up with one of our last cases of MRE's and threw the whole thing down to her. The little girl seemed stunned to have a Bradley so close and have them throw her a box of food that was nearly as big as she was. Some of the bigger kids started towards her, but stopped fast when I swung the turret on them. The little girl headed for the tree line as fast as she could carry/drag the case. We moved back to the road when we saw a woman dash out and grab the little girl. I still occasionally have dreams of that pretty little face with blood running out of her nose and down her chin after that boy hit her. What do you say when you see the face of the true victims of war. Can a box of MRE's pay some of my debt to the innocents? Is that why the LT gave her the whole case? The press seems to focus on what the government wants, not on the innocent lives spilled in the name of peace. Children should never have to suffer for adult's stupidity. I would have thought that the memory of the killing soldiers would be the subject of my nightmares, which must be buried too deep

Desert Storm

in my subconscious, but instead, it's that little girls face. It still makes me cry.

Burned out Iraqi Tank, Russian made T-72. We didn't know about the dangers of being close after depleted uranium shells had been used on it.

On a different day, we took a pickup and trailer of water off of some fleeing Iraqi troops. The orders were to not take the chance that food stuff could be poisoned. When you are thirsty and hungry, you do what you can. It was nice having water again. Some rules, you have to break to survive.

I don't remember where I was when we heard the war was over. We were still there and the enemy was still dangerous, so it

Desert Storm

meant little to us. Our next orders were contradictory to the claim of peace. General McCaffrey came over the radio and announced to us that we were about to do the first right thing in a war; that was to finish it the first time threw and we were all headed to Baghdad. All of a sudden, we were supplied with all the food, water, and ammunition we could carry and were turned north. I know we sat for more than a week, but I don't remember how long for sure. Planes were flying all over Iraq dropping leaflets telling the people to stand up against their government and we would be there to back them up. Together, we would give them freedom from oppression. Just when we started hearing about fighting breaking out all over Iraq by civilians, we got orders to destroy all our ammo and return to Dammam for going home. They didn't want us returning with full loads of ammo. The war was definitely over this time, or as we later found out, just postponed till Iraqi freedom after 9/11. As much as I wanted to go home, I felt so bad for all the people who were revolting against their government, thinking we had their backs. I love my country, but I felt that my government was out of control and had set them

Desert Storm

up to die. Later, I heard that Saddam slaughtered thousands as a warning to anyone else and to make a point to the U.S.

Much later, I heard Bush Jr. us that slaughter as one of the excuses for attacking Saddam after 9/11. In my opinion, if it was worth some of the justification for starting another war over, Bush Sr. should have been tried for crimes against humanity for setting those people up to die. No wonder they wouldn't help us during Iraqi freedom. How does that saying go, "Once burned, twice shy?" I don't blame them for not trusting our government again.

Getting rid of the ammo turned out to be another adventure in human stupidity; starting with mine. All the companies' ammo was unloaded by a big hole that had been dug where we were, before we got there. It looked like what we do to dig places for tanks to hide in; leaving only the turret sticking above ground level. I then made sure each vehicle and individual's weapons were cleared of ammo for safety as they unloaded the ammo from the Bradley.

How I was supposed to get rid of it was up to me. We had two days before we left. I decided to let my platoon get the fun of

Desert Storm

helping me "blow shit up." That was my first mistake. It started off OK, there were about five of use pulling pins and tossing grenades down into the hole to listen to them go off. I heard a Hummer pull up to the Bradley's behind us, and watched some officer and our CO go off to talk. His driver came wandering over to see what we were doing, as if you couldn't tell. My biggest mistake came when he asked to throw one. I thought, he has to know how deadly they are and that these are not toys. He should have gotten the grenade training in basic training. Where we were standing, there was a small ditch right in front of us and a small hill climbing up about waist height before it dropped into the hole, maybe about a 15-20 foot throw. Not a hard throw for a baseball grenade. This guy walks over where everybody had been throwing, pulled the pin, and limp wrists it almost straight into the air. I could see it wasn't going to make it and yelled "GRENADE" at the top of my lungs. All infantry knows what that means and dove for cover. Not that there was much cover. I had to tackle the driver because he really had no idea what he had done wrong and was standing there with a dumb look on his face as the grenade cam rolling back at him. We were just lucky

Desert Storm

enough for it to have rolled into the little ditch in front of us before it went off, and it diverted the force upward instead of out. We just got a little dirty. I thought we were all going to die. After it went off, I pulled him to his feet. My first thought was to hit him or throw him in the hole. I finally managed to get out "Get this asshole away from me." Two people jumped to grab him. I had to take a long break.

After eating and drinking a jug of cold coffee mixed with a chocolate package (our normal pick me up), I felt up to finishing. Only two of the guys went back out with me. The other two were still pretty shaken about how close we came to all dying; killed after the war is over. We finished up with the grenades pretty quickly and started on the shoulder fired rockets. We had two kinds, the small Laws and the AT-4's. I had the guys aim for a big burm to get practice on. We hardly ever get to shoot live rounds. Just to the right of the burm and about a quarter mile or more away was a petroleum storage tank farm. Dennis started to aim for the burm and then just before he pulled the trigger, he turned and fired at the nearest tank. As it went straight for the center of the tank, I thought, I guess this is the day I am to die. Instead of a

Desert Storm

big explosion, it just popped a hole through it and we could see the sun shining through. It was empty. After that, I had the guys help me throw it all into the hole and I finished the demo by myself with explosives. It wasn't as much fun this way, but C4 and Detonator Cord can be fun too. I was well away when it all went up. Now that was a big explosion.

Getting back to Dammam was a blur. We pretty much drove straight back through to the "Highway of Death" bordering northern Saudi Arabia. I didn't have to scan for enemy, so I watched the scenery go by. I just knew one of those wadies out there was where I left half my brain stuck to the sights.

When we got back to the highway, we loaded back on to trucks to take us straight into Dammam. They stopped every once in a while for us to get a chance to stretch, eat, take a bathroom break, and then we were back on to the road. We got all the junk food and candy we could eat at each stop. I slept the rest of the time. We did get informed somewhere along the way that our unit had gone further and faster than any armored unit in history. It just rattles me to know it was to stay alive because our

Desert Storm

government failed us and we would have died out there if we hadn't. It seems to take away from the notoriety.

I think we only spent a couple of days cleaning our vehicles to ship them home. The Saudis put us up in some really nice three bedroom apartments. There was no furniture, but it was cool and had hot water.

I did go in to see the sights of Dammam one evening. Other than trying the food, I didn't see anything of interest. I was too afraid of doing something wrong and have the religious police cut off a hand or cut out my eyes if they thought I had stolen something or looked at one of their women.

If anyone has asks me about the Saudi's, the only three things I can remember the most are, too much mango, don't look at the women, and all the children yelling "High GI" as we were coming in and "Fuck You GI" on our way out. We saw very little of them in-between. Because of the malice in their voices, I would suspect other units were much nearer and had more of an impact on the public than we did.

I was ready to go home. I did get to talk to my family and let them know I was alive. It was the first time since the war had

Desert Storm

ended. The relief in my parents and Mary's voice made me feel sorry for them. I can only imagine what the stress had been like for all of them. People seem to focus on the soldiers, but what about the families who live day to day, wondering if today is the day they get told their loved one is coming home in a box.

Desert Storm

Home- March 1991

We flew from Saudi Arabia to Germany and had a short layover there. I called to let everyone know I was on my way home. My mom informed me that Mary had been driving up to the military base almost every day to see if I had arrived. It was taking a toll on her to find that I wasn't there each day. I was touched. That is a 45 minute drive each way. I couldn't wait to see her. I thought, this girl must really love me.

We touched down at the Air Force base in Savannah, GA on March 21st 1991. Buses picked us up at the airfield to drive us back to the Army Base. As we approached Fort Stewart, the driver had been playing music from a local radio station. The DJ came on and welcomed us home and played *Thin Lizzy's - The boys are back in town*. It finished as we pulled up to the parade field on base. It felt good to be home. We had just been to war and came home to tell about it. We formed up on the far side of the field from the stands and marched across the field. Everyone was walking proud with our heads held high. The stands were packed with family and friends. For once, the officers were real nice;

Desert Storm

they said a short welcome home and then released us for the next four days.

I didn't see Mary anywhere in the stands. She would have been the only one there to welcome me home. Since I didn't see her around the stands, I headed for the parking lot. She had my car, so I figured I could at least find it. As I was headed to the parking lot, I saw her with her head down walking in front of me. As I caught her and spun her around, I could see she was crying. She had thought I had not been in this group to come home. As I pulled her into my arms, I asked her to marry me. To this day, I am not sure why I did that other than I was so touched and got caught up in the moment. We got married the next morning by the Justice of the Peace down in Kingston, Georgia. For a honeymoon, we drove Wally Waters down to central Florida to his family and took our time going home. We found out that Sean got married to Betty the day after us.

The day we went back to work, I approached the CO again about some of the things I saw that had disturbed me. He had me talk to someone from battalion who said he would look into it. Later that day, I found out I was chosen to go to the victory

Desert Storm

parades in Washington D.C. and New York City. There was about forty of us from different companies in the battalion.

The parade in D.C. was very formal since it was in front of the president. Because of what happened to us and the poor people of Iraq who got slaughtered, I wanted to flip him off instead of salute him as we went by. I am sure that would not have gone well for me.

Most people were really nice, especially the Vets. Some of the Viet Nam vets told us that they were living vicariously through us for the welcome home. I didn't have to buy a meal or a drink all day. Everybody wanted to pay for us. There were those people who were rather rude though. They seemed to take out their frustration about war on us, the soldiers.

New York was completely different. Everything was casual. Ticker tape was flying everywhere and girls were running into the streets to kiss the guys. Nothing can prepare you for a ticker tape parade in New York City. It seemed like controlled insanity. After the parade we were given a big dinner aboard an aircraft carrier tied up to the pier and then we were released to see the city. Since I had never been there before, I had to go up in the World Trade

Desert Storm

Center to say I had been there. I had a beer in Battle Park with some people from Queens. What a day. For both of those days, I really felt like people appreciated what I had just been through. I knew I was no hero, and felt very uncomfortable when people called us that, but I could feel proud of my accomplishments. Then back to the rest of your life where you are a no one, just struggling to get by. Did it really mean so little? I am not sure what I had expected coming home from a war, but months after the war, no one seemed to give a shit about us anymore.

Getting back home after the parades was a big letdown. I asked about the inquiry into the atrocities that I had seen, first thing when I got back and was told that an investigation was already done and no charges were filed. I threatened to take it over their heads, and they threatened to have me thrown in jail if I did not drop it. That hurt.

In college later, I learned about the Stanford mock prison study, in which a bunch of college students during the 60's went over the edge during an experiment. They physically and mentally tortured their class mates. When the experiment was stopped, the designated guards who had done the torturing couldn't explain

Desert Storm

why they went as far as they did. It devastated them that they could be so cruel. Even the people who played the prisoners didn't just quit even though they knew they could at any time. The same sort of thing happened at Abu Ghraib Prison in Cuba after 9/11. These types of incidents are all too common place to be just an anomaly, but humans don't want to admit to their shortcomings. Whether we like it or not, when put into rolls of dominance over others, it is human nature (both men and women) to inflict pain upon others to keep that control. That doesn't excuse what those guys did, but at least I finally had an explanation of how someone could do those hideous things to their fellow human. This knowledge has helped me deal with what I saw and experienced myself.

It really hurt my heart to find out that 80% of all the casualties during Desert Storm were from friendly fire. I wish there had been a bigger deal made of that. It shows the incompetent training that was being used to get us ready for a war. Our government should have been called to task for that. The soldiers should not have to pay for the government's learning curve. I know that we were never taught to identify vehicles at

Desert Storm

night, using their heat signature for the thermal sights. Half the war was fought at night with no training on how to distinguish between the enemy and us. That was just one of many deficiencies in our training.

In April, they gave us two weeks of leave. My mom and dad bought Mary, Susan and I a plane ticket to Idaho. Sean and his wife flew to Portland to be with his family. My mom had to have a church wedding for us. The Justice of the Peace didn't fit her religious beliefs. Mary seemed to be good with it. She got to wear the antique wedding dress she had. After the wedding, Mary, Susan and I drove down to Oregon to visit Sean. Mary had never seen the Northwest before, so she got to see a lot of it. It was great seeing her eyes the first time she saw Mount Hood. They don't have volcanoes in the south.

When we got back to Georgia, we went and picked up Mary's two other children. Ronald was 11 and Hanna was 13. None of the children had ever lived in the same house together before. Ronald had lived with his father, while Hanna and Susan had been bounced around from family member, to family member. That became an interesting experience. Slowly I started

Desert Storm

finding out that many of the things that Mary had told me before the war and through her letters while I was there, were nothing but lies. Taking on three kids with three daddies and a lying wife, you can see where this is headed. I was blind; she was the most beautiful, intelligent women I had ever met.

We decided to move to Idaho when I got out of the army in August of 1991. I had gone back into the military with the idea of going for retirement, but the war changed those ideas; I couldn't do something like that again. Ronald stayed with his dad and the girls and I drove from Georgia to Texas to visit more of Mary's family on our way to Idaho. We were only in Idaho for a month or so when Mary told me she couldn't stand living there and wanted to move back down to Texas to be around her brothers and sisters. One of her brothers offered to get me a job with the company he worked for, so we sold the land that I owned in Idaho and moved to Texas. We probably were not six months into my marriage, when I realized that I had made a big mistake. She informed me that the honeymoon was over. It felt like she really didn't love me at all and just needed someone to take care of her and her kids. I felt sorry for the kids. They didn't deserve to be

Desert Storm

thrown aside, so I stayed for them, and because I thought I had to. I had made a commitment in front of God and my family. What a load of crap. I now believe that God doesn't want us to suffer. I did it out of a false sense of loyalty and the false interpretations of bible scripture.

During those two years in Texas, I went to the VA and enrolled for disability because I was having trouble with my knee pain and skin rashes and sores all over my body. They gave me a zero percent disability, which meant that they acknowledged my problems, but they weren't enough to stop me from working. I also tried the Army Reserves, but my knees were hurting and swelling, and I wanted to murder the dumb shit officer in charge. What a moron. I put in my resignation. I didn't understand what was making me so angry all the time.

I also enrolled in night classes in engineering graphic and design. Working all day, dealing with raising kids and then classes three days a week put a big stress on me. I was bound and determined to make a better life for all of us.

When NAFTA went through, the chemical plant I was working at closed down and moved to Mexico. That put an end to

Desert Storm

my college also, because the company was paying for it. All over the news were reports that NAFTA did not cause any job losses in the U.S.; yah right. Because of all the unemployed people in the area, we moved back to Georgia. I had been working as a Boiler Maker/Pipe Fitter, which gave me an advantage in a job search.

The second day after we got to Georgia, I got a job as a Petroleum Pipe Fitter, doing the underground work for gas stations. I really didn't know enough to be taking the job. I have always been good at saying "sure, I can do that" and then faking it till I learned enough to make it. I needed the work to support my family.

My life felt like it was tearing itself apart. I really didn't like my boss, my job, or my life. I felt like I was digging a hole that I would never get out of. After two years of working for that company, my boss decided to screw me over on some pay, so I quit and went to work for his cousin as a foreman the next day. This company was much better to work for, but I still hated my job and was beginning to really dislike my wife and hated myself. The anger and depression kept getting worse and worse. It felt

Desert Storm

like a thorn in my soul that I could not reach; ending my life kept popping up in my thoughts every day.

My dad died in 1995. I flew home for the funeral. Dad was the last person in the family that I had, that I really felt close to and would understand at least a little of what I was going through. Don't get me wrong, I love my mom and my sisters because they are family, but I never really felt I could open up with them like I did with dad and his parents, who had died earlier in my life. Dad was the last person I felt I could really trust and now he was gone. My trust in everyone was deteriorating fast. It is hard to live in a world where the people you are supposed to trust the most, your family, are the ones that you feel are the least tolerant of you and how you feel. Then, you have to deal with a job you hate and also have to deal with how the war made you feel. It can become overwhelming very fast.

By this time, I really felt like I was losing it. I am not normally an angry person, but I had this uncontrollable urge to kill or hurt someone most of the time. I am not proud of it, but my first thought was killing Mary, but that thought passed quick, because then I would just end up in prison and still in pain. I

Desert Storm

wanted to get myself out of the pain of being alive; all alone in a room full of people.

I came home one day after work and there was a note that the kids were gone for the night. It had been a long, hard day, and I decided that it was the perfect time to put myself out of my misery. The only one who would find me would be Mary. I figured that would serve her right for what she put me through. I didn't want to be angry anymore. I pulled out my pistol, loaded it, pulled back the hammer and stuck it into my mouth. Right then, I heard the front door and Mary's daughter Susan yelling to see if anyone was home. I couldn't let her be the one to find me. I unloaded the weapon and put it away. Later that evening, I began to realize what I had been about to do and started to realize that I was completely out of control. I knew I needed a change. I did not want to seek medical help. I had seen many soldiers go in and get diagnosed with a mental disorder. I could not see myself living with that stigma. "Oh, you are mental ill, please stand over there;" like the person has some contagious disease. That was not going to be me.

Desert Storm

I went to see one of those free family counselors that had their office not too far from our house. I didn't go into much detail, and just gave some basics of my marriage. I didn't go into the anger or the suicide attempt. She asked a couple of questions about Mary and then asked me if I would like to know if Mary really did love me, which was the basic question I had about our marriage. She told me that she loved me, but her actions seemed to show a sort of disdain. I still felt that I loved her, but was angry with her and didn't want to get to the point of hating her. I was terrified about making any decision with regards to staying or leaving Mary. I didn't want to screw up again. I told the councilor, that I would really like to know. The counselor set up another appointment for next week in a time that would work for both Mary and me. She told me to tell Mary that I was having some problems and ask her if she could come to a counselor with me for my support. She was very adamant about me saying it was for me and had nothing to do with Mary other than needing her support for me. Mary's reply was "If it is your problem, then what the hell do I need to be there for." The next week at the counselor, she started out with, "Got your answer, didn't you?" I

Desert Storm

knew deep down somewhere, Mary did have some feelings for me, but we did not agree on what that looked and felt like. Maybe in her own way she did love me. Hearing her reaction did give me a clearer picture of what I was dealing with though. I knew I couldn't stay with her anymore. With a plan to leave Mary, it helped me focus.

It took me a little while to pay Mary and the kids rent ahead a couple months and to get enough for me to move somewhere. Out of my own guilt for leaving, I felt that I owed them that much. I didn't go far; I moved just out of Atlanta. That helped a little bit, but even six months later, Mary was still asking for favors, money and being a pain in the butt. I was still feeling used. It came to a head when my grandmother died. My mom sent me some money that she had left me. It was just enough to move back to Idaho. I knew that no matter how much Mary made me angry, I never wanted to hate her, but I had had enough of being used. I loaded everything I owned into a U-haul trailer and headed back to Idaho. I hated leaving the kids, but needed to get away for my own sanity. As a stepfather, I had no rights concerning the kids and two oldest were already adults. It broke my heart to leave

Desert Storm

Susan; she was my baby. I found out much later, when Susan was an adult, that her mother had neglected her after I left. I won't go into that, the details are between her and her mother. That knowledge made me feel worse for leaving her. Susan didn't deserve be neglected.

I also found out that a few months after I left Georgia, Sean left his wife and moved back to Portland with his son.

Desert Storm

Idaho

It was spring of 1997 when I got to Idaho. After being a Pipefitter Foreman for the last two years, it was easy getting another job. I started working putting in new emergency generators for the phone companies. I was mostly working by myself which was fine with me. I only had to put up with the management when I was in the office. The contract only lasted about a year though.

My next job interview, I went in for a foreman's job for a new company doing underground work for gas stations and after my first job went so well, they made me the superintendant of the company. I was used to completing stations in about two to three weeks because of the big competition in Atlanta getting ready for the 1996 Olympics, and the local standard in the North West had been six to eight weeks. They fired almost everyone and had me start training new people who wouldn't have bad habits already. I couldn't believe it took them six to eight weeks to do a job. I don't think I could have wasted enough time to draw it out that long.

Desert Storm

Part of it was the Good Ole Boy club. The subcontractors would just do whatever they felt like, any time they felt like it. I put a stop to that quick. I started asking them what they could do for me that day, and then I made them stay until they finished it. How dare I hold them to stand up to their word!! It didn't take long for them to quit trying to bullshit me and just tell me the truth. If they didn't like it, I fired them. By knowing what was going on, I could schedule to be more efficient. It got me a bad reputation with subcontractors, but my bosses and the owners of the stations loved me.

I also saw things I could do to streamline, that they wouldn't let me do in Atlanta; "It's not done like that here in Georgia." I put this new company in the black the first year. At the beginning of the second year, one of the owners, who was my direct boss, decided he knew more than I did and bid some jobs that never should have been bid. He then got mad at me because it could not be done the way he bid it. Then, he told one of my crews to change the grade mark for the levels of everything at the station they were working on. When I found out about it, it was too late to change anything and rain would run across the lot and

Desert Storm

into the front door of the store. When he told me to fix it, I told him to shove it up his ass and quit. They had the audacity to call me six months later because they were in the red again. I walked away from the whole business. I had had enough of working for big corporate assholes. It was nice to know that I could work that far up in a company, and be that valuable, even though they wouldn't admit it. It felt like a double edged sword; on one side, it helps the self esteem when everything else is falling apart to know you can accomplish something, and on the other side, my trust in people was getting worse. I was losing belief in the general honesty of mankind.

For years after, I bounced from job to job. I have gained a lot of talents over the years as far as construction goes. I am a jack-of-all-trades and master of none. The jobs usually aren't bad; it's the people I had to put up with. At least that was my perception at the time. I just knew I had to be a different species, because I didn't care for humans very much. Greed seemed to control everyone around me.

During my last year in the petroleum business, I did find out about hand drumming. My roommate took me to a dinner

Desert Storm

party with some of her friends to get me out of the house. I tended to isolate myself when I wasn't working. After dinner they all pulled out drums and put one in front of me and told me to play or leave. I tried to refuse, but they said that that was not an option. It was too long a walk back to town so I hit on it one handed the whole night. I started out angry about it, but by the end of the evening, I got to thinking, when was the last time I had felt so calm? I couldn't remember.

The next day, we were at an arts and crafts festival on the city beach and there was an African style drum and dance troupe performing. For some reason, I turned to my roommate and told her that that was what I was going to do for the rest of my life. She just laughed and told me I needed to learn to play first. I have no idea what possessed me to say that; one of those mysteries of life. At the end of the performance, they advertised for drum lessons. I jumped on it.

Drumming started with classes once a week. I used my practice time each day to take out my frustrations and anger. My teacher told me I was a little heavy handed, and needed to work on my timing. I realized I was working twice as hard to get half as

Desert Storm

far as everyone else in the class, but my moods were improving, so I ignored his comments.

I took a job in Portland with Sean for a couple of months, putting in a heating and air-conditioning unit in a warehouse. While I was there, I bought a good African Djembe from "Rhythm Traders," and got a free lesson from their Djembe Master. He told me my timing would come in time, and that playing heavy handed was just what I needed at the moment to work through for my healing. I hadn't said anything about what I had been going through to him, but it impressed me that he knew it was healing for me. That statement got me to thinking. It was more than just me that thought drumming was healing in some way.

When I got back to Idaho, my drum teacher had me start working with the beginners. He thought it would be the best way for me to learn. Every week, the students would comment about how they looked forward to their weekly therapy. A large majority of my students were single, middle-aged mothers who just needed an artistic way of dealing with their every day stress. As I learned more and more, I started seeing the potential that

Desert Storm

drumming gave for all different kinds of healing. Everyone deals with stress every day. Stress is by far the biggest killer in the world and always has been. It can cause or aggravate any human illness. When I had started, stress was my way of life.

In the summer of 1999, I got asked to sit in for a missing drummer at one of the Earth Beat Drum and Dance troupe's shows. It turned into a full time position. My drumming went from one day a week with the classes to four days a week with the troupe and classes, plus performances every other weekend. There were always six drummers (not always the same six over the years) and anywhere from eight to sixteen dancers. The average was about twelve dancers. Imagine camping out at fairs and festivals every other weekend, all summer long with eighteen people. There was a lot of growing for me. Being there through all of that experience was one of the best memories of my life. Even though there could be tension in the group at times, my anger and frustration seemed to start dropping away around my drum and dance family. In 2005, most of the people had moved away, that had been in the troupe, so we dissolved it and just kept up with the drum and dance classes. I was now the only drum teacher in

Desert Storm

town for the classes. I also played for the dance classes. That still gave me a way to stay with the drumming.

Performance at Schweitzer Ski Resort.

To my entire drum and dance family, thank you so much, it was an incredible experience. We laughed together, we cried together, we froze together, and we drummed and danced with all our hearts. You taught me that there is hope for humanity, and that there are people who can be trusted and are there to help in any way they can, with nothing but an open heart. Again, Thank You. Having a family that wants nothing more from you, than for you to be the best

Desert Storm

you that you can be, touched places in me I had forgotten that I had. I know that all good things come to an end, but it still left a hole in my heart when it ended.

I have heard that the mind of a soldier can get addicted to the adrenaline rush of combat, and felt personally that there would never be a rush like that again until I started performing with the troupe; that had been a much better and safer rush and filled that adrenal hole.

North Port, WA fair

Desert Storm

Drumming gave me an outlet for my frustration, my anger and gave me a way of expressing myself that was so creative and fun while getting me out around people again. With most everyone gone, I started feeling like I needed and was ready for a change again.

Desert Storm

Next Change

On July 1, 2006, I was working as a carpenter when the scaffolding I was working from collapsed with me on it. I fell two stories and barely missed landing on some huge rocks which were being used for landscaping. As soon as I tried to roll over, I realized I was hurt bad. I didn't know it then, but I had crushed one of the vertebras in my back. As I was waiting for the ambulance, I realized I had a decision to make. I had been learning about changing ones thoughts and changing the outcome of situations, and decided rather than taking this as a tragedy, that I would take this as a gift. To control the pain, I started making jokes with the other workers and the ambulance staff. It has always been my way to deal with physical pain by laughing, and emotional pain, by working.

When I heard the diagnosis, I knew I would never be doing construction again. I had an L3 burst fracture with no real hope of repair that wouldn't cause more problems later. Here was the next life changing experience that I had been looking for. Be careful what you ask for.

Desert Storm

The day I got home from the hospital, I got the letter from the VA saying that my veteran's disability had been increased up to 20% for my degenerative knees, which made me eligible for Vocational Rehabilitation. I had been having trouble with my knees since I had gotten back from Desert Storm and had applied for an increase the year before.

The whole time I was down recovering, I kept repeating that this was going to be one of the best things that ever happened to me. My friends were sure that I had hit my head also. I had read many self help books over the years, but they always seem to leave something out. During my drumming, breathing, and the meditation that I had started up again, I began to fill in some of the gaps in the self help books. It seemed to help me get a clearer picture of what was going on with and around me. Again, it was one of those things that I just seemed to know, but couldn't explain why I knew it.

First of all, you can't just keep telling yourself, I'm OK, I'm OK, while the other part of you is going Bullshit, Bullshit. It creates a form of cognitive dissonance. Some of my research I did when I when I went to college, was into cognitive dissonance and how it affects our lives. Cognitive dissonance is the confusion you get when what you are hearing, seeing and/or feeling doesn't fit with what you think you know about truth and reality. The mind does one of three things; it either rejects it outright (sorry, never happened), changes the story to fit its reality and truths, or changes its view of reality and truth. We live in a world that is what we decide it is; what we choose to perceive it as. To make any changes in ourselves, I realized, we need to look at the things that are causing this cognitive dissonance in us. We also have to look at "what is," which is left completely out of the self help books. What I mean by 'what is,' is looking at what and how the incident makes us feel at that moment. Denying your present state of perception, leads back to the dissonance. We first have to accept what is. It is what it is, but then we can go ahead and form creative steps towards change. Those changes will come in the future, so it has to be phrased into the future. After crushing my back, I used "I accept that I am hurt and in pain, but I choose to believe it will all work out towards my benefit." By phrasing it this way, I am accepting the now (what is), the pain, frustration, and not creating the dissonance which would slow down any recovery. I actually healed quicker than the doctors expected and to this day I don't have residual pain from the crushed vertebra, unless I do something stupid like lift more than I am suppose to or just overwork myself. I pay for those days.

My life did get better. I got accepted for the Vocational Rehabilitation program. The VA paid for four years of college. They even let me study what I wanted; music, psychology, and mind/body medicine. I met the love of my life, and got to start my own business helping others with their stress issues using drumming and percussion. It is a long way from where I was to where I am now.

I still have issues with some anger, depression, anxiety and most humans, but at least now, it doesn't dominate my life. If I have a hard day, I can breathe deep, work out my frustration and anger on the drums, and the world can disappear; at least for the moment. The biggest thing I have learned through this whole experience is that the more I know, the more I find that there is for me to know. Life seems to be about letting my experiences shape me without controlling me.

Desert Storm

College-2009

Going back to college full time at 49 was a big jump for me. I graduated high school with a C- and wasn't sure if I was up to it. I knew that this would be the only way for me to get ahead in life. Without a degree of some type, I would be just another broken down vet, struggling to get by.

I started with wanting to help a friend out with his company which used rhythm and percussion in schools. He was great with facilitation, but felt someone in his company with a college degree would support his business. Before I could get through my first two years of college he closed his company and moved. This is where I had a short time to decide on a different path for my life. I started looking into working with vets and my own struggles with the war. Rhythm Meditation Therapy (RMT) came out of that research. I found an incredible amount of evidence for using music and meditation for stress and PTSD. It was being used in the New Age culture for working with PTSD, but that seemed to limit who it was getting out too. I wanted to gather all the evidence and take it out to the general public as a solid science.

Desert Storm

The first two years I mostly worked on core studies and got my Associate's Degree with emphasis on music from South Puget Sound Community College. The next two years I spent at The Evergreen State College working on my Bachelor's Degree in Mind/Body Medicine and Psychology.

One of the things that college showed me was that just because you have a degree does not make you infallible. Several psychology professors told me that they were really disappointed in their chosen profession. When people spend so much time and money on their education, they can get caught up in what they were taught in school and not see that it really doesn't work like they were taught when they got out using their knowledge in the public realm. Some clinicians seemed to know that the methods that were taught to them were of little to no help on some things even though they worked wonders for other, but some clinicians spent so much time and money on their education, they will defend it with their every breath. Other clinicians that see the problem and are looking for options and feel that we need to change strictly to Mind/Body treatment. Other clinicians wanted to see both old and new used. Sounds like that cognitive

Desert Storm

dissonance that I talked about earlier about the mind rejecting evidence when it doesn't fit with what we thought we knew as truth. The debate is ingoing.

All of my professors were very interested in the RMT that I was developing for stress and stress related issues and encouraged me the whole way. PTSD and chronic stress have been shown to cause physical changes in the brain. These changes are damage to parts of the brain which control our chemical, electrical and cognitive functioning. RMT involves a fourfold response to that damage by targeting the damage and not just focusing on the symptoms. By working on the damaged areas first, the work on the symptoms is much more efficient.

First, the body can sometimes get stuck in the fight or flight mode, which over time, causes the damages. The body's natural recovery system (which is being suppressed by the fight or flight system) needs to be reactivated. Most of that is about teaching the body to relax again. You laugh, but it sounds so much easier than it is. People can think they are relaxed and real calming can feel uncomfortable because of the brains constant conditioning to the stress. Participating in rhythm and music naturally relaxes and anchors it in the body.

Next, it promotes the growth of new neurons around the damaged portions of the brain. All symptoms of PTSD come from that neural damage. Getting your bodily functions back running under their own regulation again is essential for any recovery.

Third, RMT allows for the release of pent up frustrations and angers in a creative, non-destructive way, and forth, it brings people together in a safe social environment without having to put you in front of a group and calling attention to yourself. That is important because most people with PTSD or chronic stress tend to isolate themselves away from other people. It is a symptom of the neural damage, but needs to be addressed.

There has been scientific study after scientific study, showing the benefits of using meditation and rhythm for healing of stress related issues that show much more evidence than the research done by pharmacology or some psychologists talk therapy.

Pharmacology can stabilize, but was never meant to reverse the damage and allow healing. By artificially stimulating the body and mind to respond using drugs, it doesn't allow the body to return to its own natural healing state. The body becomes conditioned to rely on the drugs for regulating its chemical responses rather than its own natural healing response. Yes, stabilization is important, but then the treatment needs to work towards moving the body back to its own natural regulation. By only treating symptoms, our bodies stay damaged and become more reliant on the drugs and doctors.

Psychologists are now seeing the potential of mindfulness meditation. The Veterans Administration is now offering Mindfulness Meditation programs, which is great, but you usually have to ask about it or they won't mention it. Physical response is also needed along with bringing people back into social environments. A whole body approach is needed. By combining rhythm and meditation we can work to a whole body approach to reversing the damage that was done. If you would like to know more about this, I refer you to my book *Rhythm Healing: PTSD, Trauma, and Beyond*.

People ask all the time, can you get me or my family member back to the way they were before. I have to tell them no.

Desert Storm

Never will anyone who has had PTSD or chronic stress ever be the same as they were before. With the experience that the people have that causes the damage and the re-growth of new neurons, we can never be exactly like we were before, but RMT can put us into a state that allows us to create a new self, which will be a life that we can live with rather than struggle through.

Desert Storm

Epilogue

It is a challenge that every soldier goes through after being in combat. It is a challenge that breaks many. The challenge of working through relationships, work, everyday life; and also coming to grips with who you are now, after what you have been through. I know I did not come back the same person that I was. I don't believe you can be part of something like that and not come home unaffected. Yet, our society rewards those who don't seem to be negatively affected and diagnoses those who do seem effect as being mentally deficient. Where is the justice in that? I did my job to the best of my ability and filled my obligation to this country, but I did not sign up to be used and abused by a country that says it is looking out for my best interests. I know better than that now. It seems to me that our government is- of the money, by the money, for the money; to hell with those without. This is my reality. I am currently working on letting it all go. When I struggle, nothing changes. It is when I let go that change comes.

After years later, I have worked through a lot of my mental issues, not that I am exactly where I want to be, and I am still

Desert Storm

having physical issues which can only be logically explained by years of toxicity that I picked up somewhere through my life. The most significant example that could have caused any of it was from what our government did to me and the environment that I was in during the war. These examples include depleted uranium rounds, medical shots, living environment (includes no laundry, no showers, no sleeping facilities, smoke from fires, and chemical and biological weapons) and the constant stress for months on end. Any one of those is bad by itself, but together, can be compounded by the effects of each other.

Over the years I have also had to come to grips with my part in combat. The feeling of doing my job to the best of my ability, and being proud of myself, and the shock that killing other human beings came so easily to me. Not just easy, but I felt joy in doing it. I was always the one who never wanted to fight, even though I was pushed into it several times in Jr. High and High School. I have always done my job to the best of my ability, and my job in the Army, was to find new and better ways of killing my fellow man. This left me with that dissonance; proud and disgusted with myself at the same time. The mental turmoil of

Desert Storm

dealing with that every day has been my burden. I want to feel good about myself, yet find myself hating everything about me and my life.

One thing that I did come up with that helps me is to not think of things as good or bad, rather than the good and evil that I was taught in my religious upbringing. No matter how we try to justify events in the world, good and bad exist together in all of us. Thinking of morality as more of a magnet helps. The positive and the negative are both part of the same scale. One is not better than the other, and we need one end to be able to appreciate and use the other. Every one of us can have good and evil inside. My readings into the bible and my studies into science have shown me that this seems much closer to the real truth than what I have been led to believe. One of my own personal moral struggles: I can be a killer and still be a good person.

I like the Native American story about the boy asking the elder, "I feel like I have two dogs fighting inside myself all the time, one good, and one bad, which one wins?" The elder replied, "The one you feed." This may not be the original version, but it was the one told to me. Both dogs will always be there, but it is the one we nurture and feed that prevails in your life. We all have good and bad within us. We cannot stop or change what happens to us in our lives, the only real power we have in this world is how we perceive the events. It isn't until we see this that we can start to take control of our lives. What we experience can be perceived in many ways. Our true strength comes when we realize that we can perceive those experiences in ways other than our initial reaction. Good things happen to us and bad things happen to us, it is our only true power in this world, to decide how we want to view it.

I have had too many mentors tell me that it is when we deny the other side exists that problems start to occur in your life. We don't have to follow the dark dog, but we do have to acknowledge that it exists or it will later turn and bite us in the butt.

Drumming is just the way it worked for me to start coming out of my dark self, but there are other ways that may work for you. The key is to find something that gets the brain to develop, and should have elements of visual, hearing and body motion all at the same time. Look how it helps children learn when all three are used. We as Americans use the alphabet song to teach our children with. Their development increases exponentially. We have to take ourselves back to the early stage of our lives and start over again: become as children.

One of my biggest struggles was getting past the stigma of having a mental disorder and finally reaching out to the Veterans Affairs. I found that my real friends didn't care and encouraged me and the people that it bothered stay away from me; I realized I didn't need them anyway.

It makes me sad to know that a lot of people actual believe that soldiers with PTSD are all violent or non-functioning because of the actions of a few. Having PTSD does not always cause people to more violence; a larger majority just close up inside themselves. That's what I did. I bottled it up inside and it was tearing me apart. It was not until I allowed myself to look for help and actually seek it that I started turning my life back around. As much as I wanted to be just left alone in my misery, I realized I needed others to have a life. I have swallowed my pride and done what I needed to do to live a fuller happier life. Stigma is still one of my many fears that I am living with. I let my fears influence me, but I no longer try to let them define who I am. The war that

Desert Storm

still rages inside my head is quit for the moment, but it is not gone. It colors what I see and effects what I do every moment of my life. I just don't need it dominating my life through that fear.

Thank you for taking this journey with me. It was a good way of organizing things in my own mind about my past and helped clarify things I am still working on. I hope that others can take what I have learned and find their own way of healing.

May you all be blessed on your life's journey.

Buddha-The potential in me sees the potential in you.

Desert Storm

Bill Moore, RE

SoulDance Rhythm Therapy

www.outlawdrummers.com